Unwrapping the Greatest Gift

A FAMILY CELEBRATION OF CHRISTMAS

ANN VOSKAMP

Bestselling Author of *The Greatest Gift*

Tyndale House Publishers, Inc.
Carol Stream, Illinois

Visit Tyndale online at www.tyndale.com.

TYNDALE and Tyndale's quill logo are registered trademarks of Tyndale House Publishers, Inc.

Unwrapping the Greatest Gift: A Family Celebration of Christmas

Copyright © 2014 by Ann Voskamp. All rights reserved.

Cover and story opener illustrations by Jacqueline L. Nuñez. Copyright © Tyndale House Publishers, Inc. All rights reserved.

Original cut paper illustrations by Paula Doherty.

Cover and interior snowflake pattern copyright © hoverfly/Shutterstock. All rights reserved.

Interior story illustrations copyright © Martina Peluso. All rights reserved.

Author photograph taken by Molly Morton-Sydorak, copyright © 2012. All rights reserved.

Edited by Stephanie Rische

Designed by Jacqueline L. Nuñez

Published in association with William K. Jensen Literary Agency, 119 Bampton Court, Eugene, Oregon 97404.

Unless otherwise indicated, all Scripture quotations are taken from the *Holy Bible*, New Living Translation, copyright © 1996, 2004, 2007, 2013 by Tyndale House Foundation. Used by permission of Tyndale House Publishers, Inc., Carol Stream, Illinois 60188. All rights reserved.

Scripture quotations marked NIV are taken from the Holy Bible, *New International Version,® NIV.®* Copyright © 1973, 1978, 1984, 2011 by Biblica, Inc.® Used by permission of Zondervan. All rights reserved worldwide. www.zondervan.com.

Scripture quotations marked NCV are taken from the New Century Version.® Copyright © 2005 by Thomas Nelson, Inc. Used by permission. All rights reserved.

Scripture quotations marked ESV are taken from *The Holy Bible*, English Standard Version® (ESV®), copyright © 2001 by Crossway, a publishing ministry of Good News Publishers. Used by permission. All rights reserved.

Scripture quotations marked NKJV are taken from the New King James Version.® Copyright © 1982 by Thomas Nelson, Inc. Used by permission. All rights reserved.

Library of Congress Cataloging-in-Publication Data

Voskamp, Ann, date.
  Unwrapping the greatest gift : a family celebration of Christmas / Ann Voskamp.
    pages cm
  ISBN 978-1-4143-9754-2 (hc)
1. Advent--Prayers and devotions. 2. Families--Religious life. I. Title.
BV40.V675 2014
249--dc23

Printed in China

20	19	18	17	16	15	14
7	6	5	4	3	2	1

Contents

Your Invitation to Unwrap the Gift

In the beginning—that is when this story begins. Which is far better than a story that begins with any old "once upon a time." This story is better than the greatest fairy tale you've ever heard—because this story is all true. And this story is our story—your story.

Your story starts with a kiss. That's how God made people: He gathered up some dust and dirt. He shaped and sculpted the dirt into what looked like a person— eyes sort of like your eyes and a nose kind of like yours and a mouth a lot like yours—and then the one real God, the Father-King of the whole universe, knelt close and closer and closer until His very breath breathed on our skin, and His life and love filled us until we were warm and fully alive!

Your story begins with a kiss, because your Father-King knows that the greatest gift your heart really wants and needs is love—to feel the safe, forever warmth of His love.

See how everyone everywhere is putting up Christmas trees—tall ones and wide ones and small ones? And when you open up God's love letter to us, the Bible, do you know what you find? You find the family tree of Jesus. You find the stories that trace the branches of Jesus' family, the limbs of the tree that go back to His great-great-great-grandfather and to that many-many-many-great-grandmother. And you go all the way back to the very beginning—to our beginning. And when you're tracing that family tree of Jesus, guess what you find? People who were big cheaters, bad liars, weasely sneakers, battling brothers, fighting families, and all the beaten up and brokenhearted. (Ever know any families like that?)

One of those many-many-great-great-great-grandfathers of Jesus was Jesse. And things got so rotten that his family tree looked more like the stump of a tree cut right off. But out of that chopped-off stump of a family tree came the miraculous impossible, right out of the stump. This budding branch—this green shoot of new hope, new starts, new freedom for the whole family— was Jesus! (Nobody was expecting that!)

If you open these pages every day of December, much like opening the flaps of a calendar counting down the days to Christmas, and you read each story of Jesus' family tree, and you hang the ornaments from each story on a little (or big or wide or tall) tree of your own, you'll have what we call a Jesse Tree—a picture of Jesus' own family tree! And you'll begin the unwrapping of the greatest Gift, the most enormous Gift, the most astonishing Gift that your heart really wants the most!

If we want our Christmas tree to really stand wondrous and full of meaning, the tree we really need to understand and be astonished by is the family tree of Jesus Christ. Because this is our story—your story.

God doesn't cut off all the big cheaters, bad liars, weaselly sneakers, battling brothers, fighting families, and brokenhearted from His family tree—He makes families just like these perfectly His! He adopts all the messy and broken and imperfect people into His tree and His story and His heart, and He gives us His family name. He gives us His absolute perfectness and makes us alive and fully free.

Jesus comes right to your Christmas tree and looks at your family tree and says, "I am your Rescuer, and I will set you free from all the brokenness and sinfulness and sadness. I'll be the Gift, and I'll take you. Will you take Me? Will you want Me?"

Who says yes? Who doesn't want to miss Jesus this year?

Who wants to wake up on Christmas morning with a heart that wants the greatest Gift the most? Who wants Jesus more than anything else?

Jesus in the manger, who makes Himself bread for us who are hungry. Jesus, the Savior in swaddlings, who rescues us from the darkness when we hold on to Him, the Light of the World. Jesus, who makes what all of us really want the most: Christmas.

Come, and don't miss Jesus. Come, and unwrap His story, the most unbeatable, unstoppable, unfailing love story—a story that is better than the best fairy tale, because it's all true.

Come, and be kissed by God and loved into the happily ever after. Unwrap the greatest Gift: the safest, warmest Love you've ever known.

Ann Voskamp

Jesse Tree Invitation and Instructions

So. It's nearing Christmas, and you'll need your Jesse Tree to wait for Jesus' coming. To come to the Christmas tree through the family tree of Christ.

Your Jesse Tree may take on a number of wondrous forms. A silhouette of a tree may be sewn or painted, cut out of felt, or quilted. It may be hung from the fridge, a wall, a door, a window.

Or you may use a small evergreen tree in an urn, a cluster of red dogwood branches in a vase, or a pot of hemlock, pine, spruce, sticks, or holly.

The ornaments can be purchased online at www.incourage.me or downloaded from annvoskamp.com (using the code JESSE) and then printed out to hang on any tree of your imagining or envisioning. Just whatever you do . . .

Anticipate Christ . . . and Celebrate Christmas, His Coming

All this Jesse Tree making? It's a bit like making your own family tree—a family tree with its arching branches of grandfathers and grandmothers, its sheltering leaves of aunts and uncles. To make a Jesse Tree is to trace the family line and heritage of your own forever family—the family of God.

Out of the stump of David's family will grow a shoot.
ISAIAH 11:1

DECEMBER 1
The Place Where Love Grows

TODAY'S READING: ISAIAH 11:1-2, 10

Out of the stump of David's family will grow a shoot—

yes, a new Branch bearing fruit from the old root.

And the Spirit of the LORD will rest on him—

the Spirit of wisdom and understanding,

the Spirit of counsel and might,

the Spirit of knowledge and the fear of the LORD. . . .

In that day the heir to David's throne

will be a banner of salvation to all the world.

The nations will rally to him,

and the land where he lives will be a glorious place.

Once, in the truest story that you have ever heard, His-Story, which is really your very own story, there was this family—Jesse's family. A family that was like yours, like a tree with branches of these relatives and those brothers and those sisters—a family that loved each other and hurt each other and forgave each other and failed each other. A family that failed God.

And in failing God, they fell away from closeness with God. They failed and fell and were like a fallen tree.

Their family tree was a fallen tree.

When their family tree crashed to the ground, it crushed all of their hearts.

The stump—and all of their days—felt utterly hopeless. Like their hearts had been cut right out of them.

But it happened: the wondrous impossible. It came right out of that chopped-down stump—the miracle no one ever dreamed of. Except for God. God never stopped dreaming of the miracle, the one He'd dreamed right from the very beginning, because love never stops dreaming of a way to draw close again.

If you slowed and looked very close, you could actually see it, coming straight out of that family tree that had been cut right down—a miraculous shoot was springing up out of the stump! A tender and vulnerable green shoot was growing hope again! Growing love again!

Out of the stump came one tender branch that would grow right into a crown of thorns, right into a rugged cross, right into a ladder—your ladder back to God. Out of the stump of Jesse's family tree—out of the stump of every family tree—comes the shoot of Jesus' forever-love. Jesus would go to impossible lengths to rescue you.

Jesus' love had to get to you in a big world, Jesus' love had to come to you in a loud world, Jesus had to break into the world and rescue you with a love that would always wrap safe around you. So Jesus slipped into the world as tiny as a searching green shoot, as small as a reaching new baby. Jesus comes as your little-yet-big miracle, who whispers to you in a noisy world: "Right where you are, look for the small glimpses of My love unfurling around you like a slender leaf, like the branches of a tree, like the seeking limbs of a babe."

Look for the little child everyone else forgets. Look for that hunchbacked old man no one else remembers. Look for the small, broken cracks in the world, in hearts, that would be easy to walk right by—and right there, slip in a little word that grows great courage. Miracles happen whenever we speak words that make souls stronger. Miracles happen whenever we look for shoots of Jesus' love everywhere—because this grows deep roots in Jesus' love for everyone. Miracles happen in the drawing close to the little people, the least people, the lonely people, the lost people—because this is drawing close to Jesus. This is how we all draw love everywhere.

Once, even now, there was this family who slowed down and bent down and could see small, wondrous, impossible things—that no stump is ever just a stump.

A stump is always just a place for love to grow, this small unfurling of miracles.

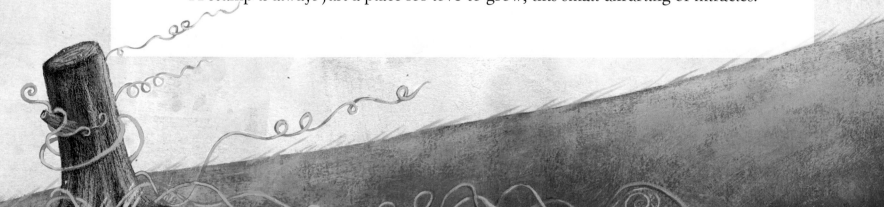

Thoughts to Discuss

How do you think God wants us to treat the less popular or less loved kid?

Who in your life needs to know that God loves them?

When have you found hope in a really hard situation?

Family Activities

Plant wheat or grass seeds today. Water them and watch them grow throughout this Advent season. Discuss how your life is like those growing seeds.

Think of small ways you can help people this December. Keep a prayer list for the people you want to show love to, and ask God to use your small actions to produce great results.

As you hang today's ornament on your Jesse Tree, say a prayer for those who are less valued in our world.

God created human beings in his own image.

GENESIS 1:27

DECEMBER 2

Created by Love

In the beginning God created the heavens and the earth.

The earth was formless and empty, and darkness covered

the deep waters. And the Spirit of God was hovering over the surface

of the waters. Then God said, "Let there be light," and there was light.

And God saw that the light was good. Then he separated the light from

the darkness. God called the light "day" and the darkness "night." . . .

God said, "Let us make human beings in our image, to be like us.

They will reign over the fish in the sea, the birds in the sky,

the livestock, all the wild animals on the earth, and the small animals

that scurry along the ground."

So God created human beings in his own image.

In the image of God he created them;

male and female he created them.

In the beginning is when the greatest story ever told begins.

The story of Christmas begins in the very beginning—because Christmas is about Jesus and Jesus' love, which has been looking to hold you close since the very beginning of time.

Jesus was before time began, His voice hovering over the depths of the darkness like a mother eagle hovers over her young. Jesus was there when the voice of God breathed wonder into the darkness: "Let there be light. . . ."

And just the sound of God's voice made light dance into being, all brightness shattering the dark.

"Let there be land." And at the music of His voice, mountains roared and raised up through the oceans. And God said, "Let there be living plants, and let there be lights in the heavens, and let there be living beasts."

And at the wonder of His voice, leaves unfurled and stars spun happy and elephants trumpeted praise.

But what about when God dreamed up the very best at the very last? God did not say, "Let there be . . ." as He had for everything else. When He dreamed of a face like yours, His voice filled with the gentlest love, and He smiled. "Let *us* make human beings. . . ."

God the Father gathered close with God the Son, Jesus Christ, and God the Holy Spirit, and all the glory of the Trinity gathered close when They imagined the masterpiece of you. And God in three persons scooped a handful

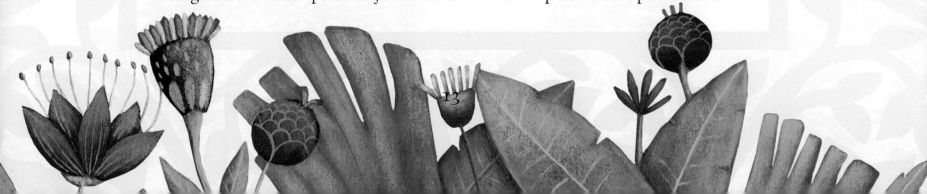

of dust together and knelt down, and together They kissed warm life into God's children with the breath of His love.

The whole world was made by God's word. But God's children alone were made by all of God's love. You were formed by a huddle of holy hearts.

You are made of both the dust of this earth and the happiness of highest heaven. You are made of both flesh and spirit, and you are made of two worlds longing for forever with Jesus.

No matter what happens in the world, the truth is always this: you were formed by Love . . . for love.

You were formed to have front-row seats to waves hugging the shore, to trees touching the sky, to stars falling across the night—the whole of the universe falling in love with God.

Your eyes were formed to be awed by the art of every wonder-laced snowflake and the carving of every swirl of frost and the sculpting of every cresting snowdrift. And then to see it—God's own signature in the corner of everything, God the artist who imagined and made the masterpiece of this world. Your mind was formed to be wowed by God. Wowed by His uncontainable, unending, unconditional, unbeatable, unfailing, unwrappable love.

You could unwrap the wow today just by going to the window. By going to the front door, to the park, to the backyard, or to the top of the highest hill you can find—standing there and staring and being wowed by the shape of clouds or the color of sky or the size of sun when you hold up your hands. You could unwrap the wow right now.

And the greatest gift we can give back to our great God is to let His love make us glad.

The whole blue marble of the world spins happy right now with the gladness of His love.

Thoughts to Discuss

What was special about the way God created humans?

How do you know God loves you?

Family Activities

Create something to show your love—cookies, ornaments, or a homemade card. Share with people who may need to be reminded that they are loved.

As you hang today's ornament on your Jesse Tree, thank God for loving you.

They hid from the LORD God among the trees.

GENESIS 3:8

DECEMBER 3

God Is Looking for You

TODAY'S READING: GENESIS 3:6-9

The woman . . . saw that the tree was beautiful and its fruit looked

delicious, and she wanted the wisdom it would give her. So she took

some of the fruit and ate it. Then she gave some to her husband,

who was with her, and he ate it, too. At that moment their eyes were

opened, and they suddenly felt shame at their nakedness.

So they sewed fig leaves together to cover themselves.

When the cool evening breezes were blowing, the man and his wife

heard the LORD God walking about in the garden. So they hid

from the LORD God among the trees.

Then the LORD God called to the man, "Where are you?"

Adam and Eve stood in awe of it, and so can we: the whole world unfolds like an art gallery filled with the glory of God. But what Adam and Eve didn't know was that there is a thief in the art gallery. An enemy of God, Satan is like a wily snake that slithers in at the corner of everything and entangles around you. And if he can trip you with a lie so you fall away from closeness with God, he can snatch your happiness, steal God's glory, swipe away your love for God, and leave you robbed.

So that snake sneaked up to Eve, wrapped his own lie tight around her, and hissed his poison right into her heart: "God doesn't really love you. God doesn't really give you good-enough things. God doesn't really give the gift of love all the time."

Eve fell for it. She ate the fruit from that one tree God had forbidden only because He loved her, because He didn't want her to die. But Eve swallowed the fruit's juice, and the snake's lie and death began to flow slow through her veins.

This is the painful loneliness that we call the Fall.

Adam and Eve ran and hid and fell away from the closeness of God.

When you trip, you can fall and end up such a bloodied mess that you go hide.

When you trip, you can fall off the path and end up lost in the long grass.

Adam and Eve hid. Adam and Eve were lost.

20

When we've fallen, and when we're lost, God comes with one question. Not the question "Why did you do that?" Not the question "What did you do wrong?" The very first God-question of the Old Testament, of the whole Bible, is a love question howling out of God's heart: "Where are you?"

God's love never stops looking for you, trying to find you and gently draw you back close to Him.

Because of His unconditional, unbeatable, unfailing, unwrappable love, your God refuses to give up on you. Your God looks for you when you're lost. Your God calls out for you when you're ashamed and broken and hurting. God doesn't run down the rebel. God doesn't strike down the sinner. God doesn't flog the failure.

Whenever you fall, whenever you fall short, whenever you sin, your God whispers to you with a love that wraps around you like a gentle arm: "Wherever you are, I will always come find you. Whatever you've done, I will always keep looking for you until My eyes see you, till My hands of healing reach you, till I can hold you close again to My heart."

No matter what the day holds, no matter how the season of your life unfolds, God holds you and enfolds you.

And what was the very first question of the New Testament of the Bible? The very first question asked in all of the New Testament of the Bible was that of wise men asking everyone after Jesus' birth: "Where is He?"

Really wise men and women never stop looking for God. And because your really wise God is love, He never stops looking for you.

At one wooden tree in the Garden of Eden, we fell for the lie that God didn't love us, and we fell away from God and got lost. And at one wooden cross near the Garden of Gethsemane, God found us and stretched out His arms and proved forever and always and no matter what that He loves us with an unconditional, unbeatable, unfailing, unwrappable love.

Sometimes you can almost feel it: when you fall, He comes and unwraps that lying, stealing snake from your feet and wraps His arms around you—and you unwrap the very greatest gift: a love that never, ever lets you go.

Thoughts to Discuss

When you feel like you've messed up and you're far away from God, what does He do?

Family Activities

Write a letter to God, thanking Him for His unconditional, unchanging love. Keep this letter beside your bed or in your Bible to remind you of His love.

Noah found favor with the LORD.

GENESIS 6:8

DECEMBER 4

God's Tears

The LORD observed the extent of human wickedness on the earth,

and he saw that everything they thought or imagined

was consistently and totally evil. So the LORD was sorry

he had ever made them and put them on the earth.

It broke his heart. And the LORD said, "I will wipe this human race I

have created from the face of the earth.

Yes, and I will destroy every living thing—all the people, the large

animals, the small animals that scurry along the ground,

and even the birds of the sky. I am sorry I ever made them."

But Noah found favor with the LORD.

You could try it—when you lean your body way to the left, or when you lean way to the right, sooner or later you're bound to fall.

And inside of every single person walking on God's globe, there beats this heart with a very bad lean to it.

Our love didn't lean toward the one real God, with His arms wide open in His uncontainable, unending, unconditional, unbeatable, unfailing, unwrappable love.

Our love leaned toward these selfish things that we made into our own fake gods—these little idols that have no real arms at all, so when we lean toward them, we just fall. Hard.

God looked at all the hearts leaning away from Him, and His bruised heart swelled with sadness.

"His heart was filled with pain" is how God felt when he looked around and saw everyone sinning and leaning and hurting (Genesis 6:6, NCV). God's tears fell like a flood.

His heart hurts not just with a few teardrops of ache, not just with a slow drip of a bit of sadness—no, the whole gigantic enormity of God's heart swells sore with what hurts your heart—and His tears of sadness flooded the world.

God leans to us who are falling in a hurting world, and He catches us. He whispers, "I love you. You know how it's almost like your mother ties her heart to your heart so that she feels what you feel? So it's almost impossible for her to forget you even for just one second? I want you to remember this down to the very deepest parts of you: it's absolutely impossible for your Father God to ever forget you, for even just one fraction of a second, because I've tied My heart to your heart even closer, and I feel what you feel, and I've written your name right here on My hand. No matter how much your earthly mother loves you—more than to the moon and back—your heavenly Father loves you infinitely more—more than to heaven and on into forever and always" (Isaiah 49:15).

God's love for you made Him weep over all our sadness and sin, and His heart filled with ache and spilled like a flood. And God offered everyone a gift, a rescue, a massive wooden ark—an ark much like a cradle on water—and He whispered, "Come to the ark."

God sees our tears now. And the hurt flooding our world right now. And He offers everyone the greatest gift—a rescue, a wooden cradle, a wooden cross—and He whispers, "Come to Jesus." Noah and his family were saved by the ark. You and the whole family on this earth are saved by Jesus alone.

Some horrible, awful, miserable, very bad days, you may look around and say, "If there's a God who really cares, He'd look at our world and His heart would break."

And God looks to Jesus, who went to the cross, that real tree, and says, "Look—My heart did break."

While Jesus hung on that cross, soldiers speared His side, as if they were piercing straight into Jesus' heart, filled with sadness for all the world's pain, and it was like the water and blood of His broken heart gushed right out—like a flood of an unconditional, unbeatable, unending, unwrappable love.

So when those floods of bad things happen, if you lean toward Jesus—if you incline toward Jesus, if you rest in Jesus—you get the Gift of Jesus, like an ark of love, holding you, carrying you, raising you gently up through any flood of sadness that fills the world.

Thoughts to Discuss

Have you ever felt God holding you up in a flood? Share how you felt.

Do you know anyone enduring a flood right now? How can you encourage that person to lean toward Jesus?

Family Activity

As a family, identify another family you think might be feeling like they're experiencing a "flood"—a time when everything seems to be going wrong. What gifts can you share with this family? Make sure to include a note reminding them that Jesus can carry them through their storm.

I will bless you . . . and you will be a blessing to others.
GENESIS 12:2

DECEMBER 5
Count the Stars

Today's Reading: Genesis 12:1-4, 7

The Lord had said to Abram, "Leave your native country,

your relatives, and your father's family, and go to the land

that I will show you. I will make you into a great nation.

I will bless you and make you famous, and you will be a blessing to others.

I will bless those who bless you and curse those who treat you with contempt.

All the families on earth will be blessed through you."

So Abram departed as the Lord had instructed. . . .

Then the Lord appeared to Abram and said,

"I will give this land to your descendants."

And Abram built an altar there and dedicated it to the Lord,

who had appeared to him.

After the flood dried up, God's tears still hadn't, because the world still ached. So God said, "I will do a new thing. I will do it through a new child. I will begin the new thing through new children and new descendants and new families and a new King and a new Kingdom."

So God—God who always keeps coming to us, God whose love never, ever, no matter what, ever stops coming for us—God came to a man named Abram.

And God said to Abram, "Leave everything—because I love you more than anything. Because I have a gift for you that's the very greatest, the most stupendous, the most enormous gift that's beyond anything you have ever dreamed of. You have to leave everything you know, and you need to trust Me with everything you have, and you'll have everything you need, because I will be with you."

God took Abram out into the darkest, blackest night and asked him to look up and believe. "See all the stars?" God asked. Abram looked up and he saw: there's always light in the dark. The stars all danced. "Can you count all those stars, Abram?"

And Abram stared into that velveted night sky, and a million, billion, trillion diamond-shimmering stars danced around him, and Abram tried to count all the ways—the thousands and millions and billions of ways—God loved him, and it made him dance in awe with the stars, with God.

"See?" God asked. "I will bless you. I will not burden you down. I will not break you up. I will bless you—because I'm the God of unconditional, unbeatable, unfailing, unending, unwrappable love.

"I will bless you," God said once, keeps saying now. "I will give you the greatest gift of love."

Did you feel the wind today? Did you hear Christmas carols playing? Did you hear someone laugh, see someone smile? These are all love gifts from God to you. The earth under where you live and the sky curving over you right now and the stars spinning all round you in their brazen glory: these are all God's love gifts for you, you, you. Can you count all the ways God loves you? Can you take the dare and count the love gifts He gives you every day? (1) lights twinkling in windows like stars; (2) softly worn pajamas; (3) all the candles on birthday cakes. Count all His gifts, all His gifts, all His gifts—and listen for God echoing through everything, everywhere: "I will bless you; I will give you the greatest gift of love."

And God promises even more: "I will make you a blessing to others. I will do more than give you a gift of love—I will make you into a gift of love!" You get to be the gift and smile for someone, you get to be the gift and laugh for someone, you get to be the gift and love someone who is needing a gentle touch.

You are blessed! You get to bless! This is happiness.

Abram followed God to the land that He showed him, believing that God would bless, believing that one day God would bless all families—your family—through a Child who would be born under one enormous, blazing, brilliant star.

The greatest gift God gives you is Himself—His very own presence.

This, too, could make you dance.

Thoughts to Discuss

This season, start a list of all the ways you are blessed. Add new blessings each day and thank God for each of them.

Family Activities

As a family, go to a neighbor's home. Be a blessing in some way—by bringing cookies, a card, or your smile.

Look for the stars tonight. Thank God for His promise to bless Abram—and to bless you!

God has brought me laughter.

GENESIS 21:6

DECEMBER 6

The Gift of Laughter

The LORD kept his word and did for Sarah exactly what he had promised. She became pregnant, and she gave birth to a son for Abraham in his old age. This happened at just the time God had said it would.

And Abraham named their son Isaac. Eight days after Isaac was born, Abraham circumcised him as God had commanded.

Abraham was 100 years old when Isaac was born.

And Sarah declared, "God has brought me laughter. All who hear about this will laugh with me. Who would have said to Abraham that Sarah would nurse a baby? Yet I have given Abraham a son in his old age!"

One . . . two . . . three . . . four . . . five. . . . Try counting all the way up to ninety-nine! That's how old white-haired Abraham was when he stood underneath all those millions of stars and tried counting them all. One . . . two . . . three . . . four . . . five—my, oh my!

Standing there under thousands and millions of blinking stars, Abraham had one question when God said He would give Abraham thousands and millions of children—as many as the stars in the sky.

How?

Abraham and his wife didn't have even one kid. So they didn't have even one grandchild. They only had one worn-out prayer that God would give them just one miracle child of their own to hold and to laugh with and to love forever.

But wait—who births the stars with the very breath of His mouth?

God does!

If God births stars, couldn't He make one old man and one old woman birth one little baby? Couldn't God grow a family into a love big enough to fill the skies?

"Abraham," God said, "everything is always more than it seems, more than you can see. I am doing unexpected things! I am sending you a child! And through that child, your family will grow big and the whole earth will be blessed."

Abraham laughed happy. And when the news of a miracle child reached the ears of his wife, Sarah, she laughed too—but Sarah laughed sad. Sarah laughed

the way you do when you think someone is teasing you, and you laugh brave so you don't cry hard. Sometimes you use laughter like a shield to protect your heart. Could Sarah let down her guard and believe that God would be gentle with her dream to hold a child of her own? Sometimes when your heart hurts, your head hurts to believe.

Many months went by. The stars came out every night. Sometimes Abraham and Sarah went out on the hillside and tried to count them all. Abraham's one hundredth birthday passed. (Can you imagine trying to blow out one . . . two . . . three . . . one hundred candles?)

And then, when Abraham was one hundred years old, Sarah had a baby—a baby boy!

Abraham leaned in close over the baby, his forehead gently touching Sarah's. "Isaac!" Abraham smiled. Isaac means "laughter." They would laugh with him and love him forever.

Sarah held little Isaac and laughed with joy to the heavens. "God has brought me laughter!" Her wrinkles and weariness melted away as her lips cradled her smile, her arms cradled her child. God brings us the gift of laughter—like bubbly, fizzy, soda-pop joy for our hearts.

Joy is the gigantic secret gift that God gives us and we never stop unwrapping. We were once all alone, but now we've been given a Child—the many-many-many-great-grandson of Abraham, the Baby Jesus. And Jesus makes us laugh because He's coming to save us and free us from all our fears.

All fear comes from thinking that somewhere God's love will end. But God's unbeatable, unstoppable, unwrappable love for you will never, no matter what, end. So we can loosen up, because all our heavy, sad chains have been loosed, and we can laugh free.

Because of Jesus, the other miracle Child who came to us, laughter

comes to us too. And we get to hold the wonder of it close to us. Sadness is not the end of the story. Jesus is the end of our story—and the beginning of our story and the best part of our story.

Because of Him, we can sing *fa-la-la-la-la* and feel what laughter does inside of us—it sends soda-pop-fizzing, bubbly joy all the way down to our toes.

Thoughts to Discuss

When was the last time you laughed a big, fizzy laugh? How did that feel?

Family Activities

Look for three chances today to make three different people laugh with you.

Abraham named that place The LORD Provides.
GENESIS 22:14 (NCV)

DECEMBER 7
Here I Am

God tested Abraham's faith. God said to him, "Abraham!"

And he answered, "Here I am."

Then God said, "Take your only son, Isaac, the son you love, and go to

the land of Moriah. Kill him there and offer him as a whole burnt offering

on one of the mountains I will tell you about." . . .

Abraham took the wood for the sacrifice and gave it to his son to carry,

but he himself took the knife and the fire. So he and his son went on together. . . .

But the angel of the LORD called to him from heaven and said,

"Abraham! Abraham!"

Abraham answered, "Yes."

The angel said, "Don't kill your son or hurt him in any way. Now I can see that you

trust God and that you have not kept your son, your only son, from me."

Then Abraham looked up and saw a male sheep caught in a bush by its horns. So

Abraham went and took the sheep and killed it. He offered it as a whole burnt offering

to God, and his son was saved. So Abraham named that place The LORD Provides.

Even today people say, "On the mountain of the LORD it will be provided."

Long ago people built altars, just stacks of wooden sticks, and laid lambs on the altar as a sacrifice, as a love gift to God. But over time people forgot about the one real God's love. They made up fake gods and said that their angry gods didn't want a lamb as a gift on the altar but demanded children instead. Can you imagine? For years, people hoped there was a real God somewhere who would come and tell them to stop sacrificing their children on the altar.

One day the one real God came and called: "Abraham."

And Abraham said, "Here I am."

And God said, "You know that very own son of yours, whom you love with your whole huge, soft heart? Come sacrifice him as a present to Me on an altar up on a mountain I will show you."

Abraham nodded a slow yes. Lay his very own miraculous child down on an altar, kill him as a sacrifice, a present, to God? Abraham didn't argue. He didn't complain. He didn't rage. The only thing Abraham said to God was, "Here I am."

When you say those three words, "Here I am," it's another way of saying another three words: "I love you."

And Abraham could feel God's love all around him. He could feel it—just like air. God's love was everywhere. Abraham trusted God—trusted that God's love would be like air and fill his lungs, would fill his hurting places, would keep his whole huge, soft heart beating brave. He trusted that God would provide another way, if he would just obey.

Early the next morning, Abraham called Isaac, and together they followed God up a mountain. In Abraham's hand was a knife. On Isaac's back was the wood. "But, Dad," Isaac said, turning, "where is the lamb for the sacrifice, for the love gift?"

Abraham breathed in deep, filling his lungs, and then he exhaled what he believed: "God will provide us with the lamb for the sacrifice, the present."

Worry is always belief gone wrong. Because you don't believe that God will get it right. Peace is belief that exhales. Because you believe that God's love is everywhere—like air.

Abraham stacked the wood. He made an altar, a place for a gift. Abraham laid his very own miraculous child down on the altar. And then his fingers gripped tight around the knife, because it was time to obey God, and he thought his whole huge, soft heart might break. But he took a deep breath, lifted the glinting, sharp edge of the knife over his child, and . . .

"Abraham! Abraham!" The one real God interrupted everything.

And Abraham exhaled relief: "Here I am." He said what he always said to God. Said those three words, just as if he were saying another three words to God: "I love you."

"Stop!" God said. "You were willing to give Me your own love gift, your only son."

But the one real God hoped to show the world that He wanted all His miraculous children to be living presents to Him, to be living sacrifices, living gifts. The one real God wanted all His children to say every day to Him, to people in need, those three words: "Here I am"—which is another way of saying three other words: "I love you."

And there in the thicket, a ram bleated. Abraham picked it up, just like picking up a present, and he laid the ram on the altar. Everywhere, everywhere, God provides presents! Just like many years later, God's own miraculous Son would carry a wooden cross up a hill to be our very own Lamb—the most miraculous present to the whole world.

The whole world is breathing in air everywhere right now, breathing in the love of God.

Thoughts to Discuss

What would it look like for you to trust God with your whole heart today?

Family Activities

As a family, make a list of ten different ways God has provided for you. Put the piece of paper under the Jesse Tree as a reminder that God is your Provider.

Surely the LORD is in this place, and I wasn't even aware of it!
GENESIS 28:16

DECEMBER 8
Climbing Up

TODAY'S READING: GENESIS 28:12-16

As [Jacob] slept, he dreamed of a stairway that reached from the earth up to heaven. And he saw the angels of God going up and down the stairway. At the top of the stairway stood the LORD, and he said, "I am the LORD, the God of your grandfather Abraham, and the God of your father, Isaac. The ground you are lying on belongs to you. I am giving it to you and your descendants. Your descendants will be as numerous as the dust of the earth! They will spread out in all directions—to the west and the east, to the north and the south. And all the families of the earth will be blessed through you and your descendants. What's more, I am with you, and I will protect you wherever you go. One day I will bring you back to this land. I will not leave you until I have finished giving you everything I have promised you."

Then Jacob awoke from his sleep and said, "Surely the LORD is in this place, and I wasn't even aware of it!"

Abraham's son, Isaac, grew up, like all miraculous, wonderful children do, and he had a son named Jacob. And Jacob was a struggler. One night during his travels, Jacob lay down on the ground and looked up at a black blanket of stars, and he dozed off into dreams. Jacob dreamed of wonders—that from his hard bed of earth, right up to the starry heights of heaven, there was a long, long ladder that stretched on and on—the way things can only go on and on in dreams.

And angels—blazing angels of light—were going up and coming down this ladder in Jacob's dream, this ladder that stretched on and on, from earth right up to heaven.

Now a ladder that reached all the long way from heaven to earth would be impossible to climb and climb and climb. Except people really do keep trying— not during dreams, but during the day. People keep trying to do enough good, climb enough steps, haul up enough rungs to finally pull their whole weary selves all the long, impossible way up to heaven. But the thing is, we live in a fallen world, and we have a tendency to fall, especially off imaginary ladders.

Yet have you seen or heard that this is the dream that comes true?

The real amazing dream is that there are no ladders to climb up at all, ever, because Jesus comes down to get you.

Jesus Himself explained the dream of Jacob's ladder that goes on and on and on: "You will

49

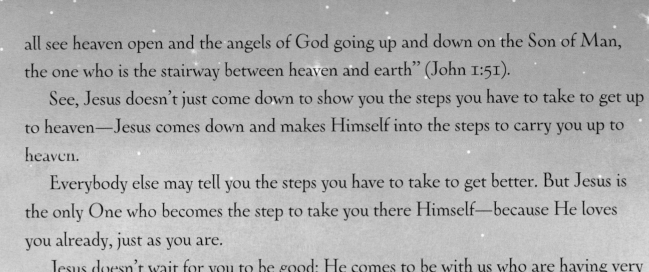

all see heaven open and the angels of God going up and down on the Son of Man, the one who is the stairway between heaven and earth" (John 1:51).

See, Jesus doesn't just come down to show you the steps you have to take to get up to heaven—Jesus comes down and makes Himself into the steps to carry you up to heaven.

Everybody else may tell you the steps you have to take to get better. But Jesus is the only One who becomes the step to take you there Himself—because He loves you already, just as you are.

Jesus doesn't wait for you to be good; He comes to be with us who are having very awful, miserable, no-good days right now. Jesus comes to carry us who are feeling mad and bad and sad and anything but glad, and He left heaven to be with us who feel left out. Jesus comes to us who seem to get every step wrong—He becomes the step just to get us.

Jesus came from heaven to be with you in your hurt.

What if, every time you looked at a Christmas tree, you could see it—how every Christmas tree looks a bit like a ladder? And Jesus is your ladder who wants to give you the gift of letting Him carry you up, no matter how far down you've fallen.

The wonder of it—Jesus picks you up at your lowest and loves you all the way up to the starry sky.

It's like waking up and discovering that all your wildest dreams have become the happiest, arm-waving true.

Thoughts to Discuss

What does it mean that Jesus is a ladder for you?

How is it good news that Jesus wants to be a ladder for you, bringing you up to Him when you've fallen down?

Family Activities

Write a note to someone to remind that person how much God loves him or her. Send this note with a Christmas card.

As you hang today's ornament on your Jesse Tree, thank God for coming down from heaven to be with you.

You intended to harm me, but God intended it all for good.

GENESIS 50:20

DECEMBER 9

Surprise Gifts

TODAY'S READING: GENESIS 37:3-4, 50:15-17, 19-20

Jacob loved Joseph more than any of his other children because

Joseph had been born to him in his old age. So one day Jacob had a special

gift made for Joseph—a beautiful robe. But his brothers hated Joseph because

their father loved him more than the rest of them.

They couldn't say a kind word to him. . . .

Now that their father was dead, Joseph's brothers became fearful.

"Now Joseph will show his anger and pay us back

for all the wrong we did to him," they said.

So they sent this message to Joseph: "Before your father died, he instructed

us to say to you: 'Please forgive your brothers for the great wrong they did to

you—for their sin in treating you so cruelly.' So we, the servants

of the God of your father, beg you to forgive our sin." . . .

Joseph replied, "Don't be afraid of me. Am I God, that I can punish you?

You intended to harm me, but God intended it all for good."

This family tree kept growing like the biggest Christmas tree where we find the greatest Gift: Adam had a baby named Seth, and Seth had a many-great-grandson named Noah, and Noah had a son named Shem, who had a many-great-grandson named Abraham, who had a son named Isaac, who had a son named Jacob, who had twelve strapping sons—including one of the littlest ones who was named Joseph. Jacob decked out his boy Joseph in a colorful coat that looked like a present wrapped up with a thousand different ribbons. When Joseph spun around in the robe, he looked like a spinning globe, all lit up with colored lights.

Joseph's brothers didn't like this. They didn't like Joseph spinning around in his colorful coat from their dad, so they schemed up a plan to weasel him out of his coat and then right out of the family. They tore the coat off Joseph, dipped its fraying hem in some blood, sold their little brother to total strangers who just happened to be wandering by, and then went home and showed the torn and bloody coat to their dad. The whole mess tore out their father's heart.

Messes and mean things can do that.

Some days, when you feel brave, you can give yourself a gift and tell someone what has torn your heart. Some days, when you feel brave, it's almost like you can reach through the pieces where your heart feels torn and touch the gentle peace of God.

Joseph, sold into Egypt by his very own brothers to be a slave, sold to strangers far away from the hug of his very own father—he got brave one day when he was in that land far away from his father's arms. It was like he felt along the torn edges of his heart and he whispered the truth he saw:

"What someone else meant for bad, God means to make it good."

No matter what tries to tear you apart, God holds your heart.

No matter what bad was meant to harm you, God's good arms have you.

You can stand around your Christmas tree with a family tree as messy as Joseph's, with cheaters and beaters and deceivers, with a family like Jacob's, who ran away and ran around and ran folks down. But out of a family that felt just like a mess, God brought Jesus, the Messiah.

Many years later, after Joseph gave his starving brothers food and they realized who this generous man really was, Joseph embraced each of his brothers with forgiveness.

God always brings good out of bad. God always turns hard things into good gifts.

One day Jacob's many-many-many-many-great-grandson would be born in a manger and wrapped in rags by His earthly dad, and He would grow up to be sold by His friends and torn apart on a cross. And God would take that greatest sadness and make it into the gladness of the greatest Gift for us. Jesus embraces us with forgiveness and rescues us from all the sin and sadness! God always takes crosses and turns them into gifts.

All the world robed for Christmas—we're loved by our Father, we who all spin around in these lit colors everywhere.

Thoughts to Discuss

Share about a time when God turned something bad into good for you and your family.

How can recalling this story help you celebrate God's love for you today?

Family Activities

Make something colorful for a friend or a neighbor. Tell that person that God loves him or her.

When you hang today's ornament on your Jesse Tree, thank God that He always brings good—even out of bad things!

> *The LORD said to me, . . . "Oh, that their hearts would be inclined to fear me and keep all my commands always, so that it might go well with them and their children forever!"*
>
> DEUTERONOMY 5:28-29 (NIV)

DECEMBER 10

Ten Love Rules

TODAY'S READING: DEUTERONOMY 5 (NIV, SELECTED VERSES)

Moses summoned all Israel and said:

Hear, Israel, the decrees and laws I declare in your hearing today.

Learn them and be sure to follow them.

"I am the LORD your God, who brought you out of Egypt, out of the land of slavery.

"You shall have no other gods before me.

"You shall not make for yourself an image in the form of anything in heaven above

or on the earth beneath or in the waters below.

"You shall not misuse the name of the LORD your God.

"Observe the Sabbath day by keeping it holy.

"Honor your father and your mother, as the LORD your God has commanded you.

"You shall not murder.

"You shall not commit adultery.

"You shall not steal.

"You shall not give false testimony against your neighbor.

"You shall not covet . . . anything that belongs to your neighbor."

The LORD said, "Oh, that their hearts would be inclined to fear me and keep all my

commands always, so that it might go well with them and their children forever!"

God knew you could get the biggest, grandest gift you can imagine, but you would never feel happiness tingling in your toes, happiness like a blanket wrapping around you warm, unless you had Him.

So God called His people close. And the people came close to the foot of a mountain so they could see the heart of God.

God took a flat stone and scratched the words of His love right into the rock. Can you imagine a love like that—so deep that it could write its love right into rocks?

Ten times God wrote it out—how He would love you, how He wanted you to love Him. You may have heard what He wrote ten times; you may have heard God's love called the Ten Commandments.

The Ten Commandments are more than God saying, "Here are My rules of law for you"; they are God saying, "Here is My real love for you."

So God wrote His love right into the rock, saying to His people, just like a man might tell his bride at their wedding,

"Here, I take you to be Mine, and you will be the one I will love more than anything—so have nothing in your life you love more than Me.

"Here, I give you My name—My very name to make you Mine— so please do not say My name without love.

"Here, I want nothing more than to spend time with you, holy time just for you and Me—so set apart one day every week for you and Me to enjoy each other.

"Here, I love you, special one—so don't want what others have, because I will give you what you need. So don't lie, because My forever-love for you means you never have to be afraid of telling the truth. So don't steal from others, because I promise I will always, always give you what you need. So don't murder anyone in anger, because My love for you will always soothe away any anger.

"Here, I love you with an unconditional, unbeatable, unfailing, unending, unwrappable love—so let's live out of our love."

All through the commandments, God etches into the stone, like a whisper: "I am the Lord your God, the Lord your God, the Lord your God. You are Mine. You are *Mine*. Make Me yours."

And a bit like at a wedding, the people of God heard God's love, and they said, "Yes, yes, You are ours, and all this we will do—we do, we do, we do."

God gives His beautiful people this great gift—these two tablets of stone with this forever love that He wrote with His very own finger. God gives the Ten Commandments as more than rules to follow—He gives them as a real love to feel.

But God knew that we would fail to keep His love commandments and we would take things that aren't ours and we would want so many things more than God and we wouldn't keep the commandments and keep close to Him. Though we said, "We do," a lot of days what we really live is, "We don't."

The heart of God hurt: "Oh, that their hearts would be inclined, would lean toward the wonder and awe of Me, lean toward keeping all My commands, because they want to keep close to My heart and my unconditional, unbeatable, unfailing, unending, unwrappable love."

God gives the love commandments to us—and God gives Himself, Jesus, to keep the love commandments for us.

Loving Jesus and loving everyone are the biggest, grandest, greatest gifts you can give back to God.

Did you know that in many places in the world when anyone recites the Ten Commandments, every listener dances with joy?

Love like this could make us wonder. Somewhere right now, Christmas carols are playing. Even right now, a love like Jesus' coming could make you dance!

Thoughts to Discuss

Why do you think God gave us the Ten Commandments?

How do these commandments show us God's love?

Family Activities

Say the Ten Commandments together. Look for God's love in each commandment, and say "I do" to God.

You must leave this scarlet rope hanging from the window.

JOSHUA 2:18

DECEMBER 11
The Red Rope

Joshua secretly sent out two spies from the Israelite camp at Acacia Grove. He instructed them, "Scout out the land on the other side of the Jordan River, especially around Jericho." So the two men set out and came to the house of a prostitute named Rahab and stayed there that night. . . . Before the spies went to sleep that night, Rahab went up on the roof to talk with them. "I know the LORD has given you this land," she told them. . . . "Now swear to me by the LORD that you will be kind to me and my family since I have helped you. Give me some guarantee that when Jericho is conquered, you will let me live, along with my father and mother, my brothers and sisters, and all their families." . . . Before they left, the men told her, "We will be bound by the oath we have taken only if you follow these instructions. When we come into the land, you must leave this scarlet rope hanging from the window through which you let us down."

A long time ago, after God gave His love promises to His people, one red rope saved the lives of a girl and her father and her mother and her sisters and her brothers. The girl's name was Rahab, and she was known as a girl who did bad things. She lived in a town named Jericho, a town where no one worshiped God. The people who lived in Jericho built high walls around their town to keep enemies out—but no one could keep out the one real God.

God told His own people that the land of Jericho would be theirs. So two men of God came spying out this land, slinking closer to Jericho, and they found the city gate standing wide open. God does that: He opens doors and opens the hardest hearts. The spies walked through the gate. They knocked on a door. Rahab let them in.

But someone saw the men slip into Rahab's house. They told the king, and the king sent soldiers. Then—quick—Rahab hid the two spies up on the roof under piles of straw. So the soldiers didn't find the spies.

When Rahab pulled that blanket of straw off the hiding spies, she whispered to them what was beating loud in her heart: "Your one real God works real miracles. I believe in Him—but even more, I want to live for Him."

God can show Himself and His huge, uncontainable love wherever, whenever, to whomever. High walls and hard hearts can't stop His love from coming. Sin and badness can't stop His love from coming. The love of God can come over any wall, can open the door of any heart, can find anyone, anywhere, in any-

thing. Rahab couldn't stop smiling. God loved her at her darkest and baddest, and He held her with the biggest and grandest and greatest love.

That is always the secret to unwrapping the biggest, greatest, grandest gift: believe that the love of Jesus is in the place where you don't expect it. Then live into the surprise of a love like that.

Because Rahab believed in the one real God and had decided to live for Him, the two men of God promised, "If you hang this red rope from your window, you and your father and your mother, your brothers and sisters, will all be kept safe when our soldiers take Jericho and God gives this city to His people."

Rahab nodded yes. She hung that red rope out her window like it was her only lifeline.

Her heart was tied to God's by that one red rope. God changed the heart of the girl who had done bad things.

When the soldiers came to take the city of Jericho, Rahab was saved—not because she was good, not because she did good things, but because she trusted the one real God.

God would send a prince named Salmon to marry Rahab. (Who was expecting that?)And the girl who had done bad things but gave her heart to the one good God became Princess Rahab, who had a baby boy who would grow up to have a baby boy who would grow up to have a baby boy who would grow up to have a baby boy—who would become the king of God's people. Which means that Rahab would be the great-great-grandmother of King David, the greatest king of God's peo-ple—and Rahab would be the many-many-many-times great-grandmother of the greatest and most perfect King ever: Jesus.

Jesus, who painted a rope red with His very own love, with His very own blood, and gives Himself to you like a red rope, whispers, "No matter what you've done, hold on—I love you, and I've got you."

Everywhere—do you see it? Christmas presents, tied-up red ribbons, little red ropes. They tie all of our hearts to Jesus, the greatest, grandest Gift.

All the red ropes everywhere shaped into hearts—they wrap the happiest love right around you.

Thoughts to Discuss

Have you ever seen God turn someone's life completely around, so that person went from choosing a bad path to following Jesus? How is Jesus doing just that miraculous thing in your life?

How is Jesus like a lifeline to you—a rope you can hold on to no matter what?

Family Activities

Look around for as many red things as you can find. When you see the color red, think of Rahab's journey of faith and the gift of Jesus.

Your people will be my people, and your God will be my God.

RUTH 1:16

DECEMBER 12

The Little Things

Naomi and her daughters-in-law got ready to leave Moab to

return to her homeland. With her two daughters-in-law she

set out from the place where she had been living,

and they took the road that would lead them back to Judah.

But on the way, Naomi said to her two daughters-in-law,

"Go back to your mothers' homes. And may the LORD reward you

for your kindness to your husbands and to me. May the LORD bless

you with the security of another marriage." Then she kissed them

good-bye, and they all broke down and wept. . . . But Ruth replied,

"Don't ask me to leave you and turn back. Wherever you go, I will go;

wherever you live, I will live. Your people will be my people,

and your God will be my God."

There was once a hungry family—a mother and a father and two big boys—and they lived in Bethlehem, which means "house of bread." But the whole family was starving—for bread, for anything to put in their bowls. So they packed up everything they owned and moved far away to live among people who had food—and false gods. They moved in next door to a girl named Ruth.

One day the father died. The mother, whose name was Naomi—she cried. Later, Naomi cried with happiness—the day when Ruth smiled yes and married one of her sons. For a while Naomi felt like her plate was heaped full of good, sweet things.

But then both sons died. Naomi's heart broke. She felt alone in all the world and hungry for love. Sometimes no one sees how lonely you feel inside. Ruth held Naomi when she cried again. Naomi said she was going to go back home. She'd left Bethlehem starving—and she was going back bitter.

Ruth was smart, standing there in the dark. She looked for the light. That's what smart people always do: brilliant people are the ones who never stop looking for the light of Jesus in everything.

"I will go with you back to your home. I will go with you and love you and look for the good, for the gifts." Ruth hugged Naomi with her smile. Ruth left the land of idols she had grown up in and went back to Naomi's land, moved to Bethlehem and that house of bread.

When Ruth returned to Bethlehem with Naomi, she just happened to end

73

up harvesting wheat in the field of the man who had the right to buy back the family land Naomi lost when she moved away from Bethlehem. His name was Boaz. Boaz just happened to meet Ruth out in his field gathering wheat, and Ruth just happened to tell him her story, and Boaz just happened to offer to help.

And Boaz just happened to say he would take Ruth to be his wife and he would buy back Naomi's family land. Guess who came to the wedding? Boaz's mother—who just so happened to be the long-ago girl who did bad things but became a princess—Rahab! (Now who was expecting that?) Naomi and Rahab both cried happy joy at the wedding. And Ruth and Boaz just happened to have a son. Naomi and Rahab were grandmothers to a little boy named Obed. And Obed happened to have a son named Jesse, who had a son named David, who became—yes, that King David, the greatest king Israel had ever known—until his many-many-many-great-grandson was born one day in Bethlehem: Jesus! The baby King who would be like bread to make sure our hearts would never be hungry for love again.

It sure didn't look like any miracles were happening in the story of Naomi and Ruth, did it? No angels appeared stage left, no donkeys started talking, no fireballs fell from heaven. But did you see that? All the little things that happened—they just happened to be little miracles. All that's happening around you every day is happening to make miracles.

Every little thing is going to be okay, because God is working good through every little thing. There is never a night, never a darkness when gifts and miracles and joy aren't coming—coming right to you.

It's a miracle in itself—how you don't have to buy any Christmas miracle at all!

The big miracle of an unbeatable, unfailing, unwrappable love is happening all around you right now.

Jesus is coming—coming like a miracle into everything!

Thoughts to Discuss

What little miracles have you seen in the past few days?

How can you keep your eyes open to notice the little things God is doing all around you?

Family Activities

Turn off all the lights in the room except the Christmas lights. Notice how the darkness makes the light seem even brighter. Thank God for being your light, even in dark times.

People judge by outward appearance, but the LORD looks at the heart.
1 SAMUEL 16:7

DECEMBER 13
Looking at Things Inside Out

When [Jesse's sons] arrived, Samuel took one look at Eliab and thought,

"Surely this is the LORD's anointed!"

But the LORD said to Samuel, "Don't judge by his appearance or height,

for I have rejected him. The LORD doesn't see things the way you see them.

People judge by outward appearance, but the LORD looks at the heart." . . .

All seven of Jesse's sons were presented to Samuel. But Samuel said to Jesse,

"The LORD has not chosen any of these." Then Samuel asked,

"Are these all the sons you have?"

"There is still the youngest," Jesse replied.

"But he's out in the fields watching the sheep and goats."

"Send for him at once," Samuel said.

"We will not sit down to eat until he arrives."

So Jesse sent for him. He was dark and handsome, with beautiful eyes.

And the LORD said, "This is the one; anoint him."

It sort of went together like peanut butter and jam: God spread out all the land around Jericho for His people—and now His people wanted Him to spread out a king's robe for them. So God gave them what they wanted: a king. But the first king, Saul, turned out to not want much of God after all. So God sent Samuel, a man who loved Him, to go find another king He had picked out—one of Jesse's eight boys. In Bethlehem.

Daddy Jesse nudged his oldest son—the one with big broad shoulders, the one who was tall enough to play basketball—and the boy stood grinning right in front of Samuel.

Well . . . surely! thought Samuel. *Surely, he looks like he could carry a big sword and wear a big, dazzling crown. He has to be the one in whom God has seen a king.*

But the Lord gently drew near to Samuel: "But look here—I don't see the way you see. You people look on the wrapping paper on the outside—but I look on the gift inside: the heart."

Huh, thought Samuel.

But Samuel wasn't alone in seeing how things look on the outside. Grannies and truck drivers and little kids and all of us—we look at the way things seem on the outside. But God looks at the way things really are on the inside. It's sort of like a sandwich: God doesn't care about the bread of the sandwich; God cares about what's in the middle.

Do you know what the laziest part of your whole beautiful body can be? Not your toes, not your belly button, but your eyes. It's like all of us need to do eye exercises every day, giving our eyes muscles to see things the way they really are. Do you know the very best exercise for your eyes? To walk with Jesus.

When you walk with Jesus, your eyes do the most miraculous things:

Your eyes go around turning everything inside out.

You start to see the realest, most wondrous things. People aren't really bodies; they are really hearts. For all our skin, people are really souls.

So Samuel tried to see the way God sees.

Daddy Jesse nudged his next son in front of Samuel, but no—Samuel shook his head. Then the next son and the next son and the next son, until there were no more sons left. Samuel was still shaking his head. "No."

"So—how about any more sons?"

"Well, there is the kid brother." Daddy Jesse sighed. "But he's a sheep watcher and a goat herder, and he's pretty puny too."

Ah, Samuel remembered. *People care about the wrapping paper on the outside, but God cares about the gift inside—the heart, which can wrap like love around everyone.*

"Go holler for him!" Samuel said. "We aren't eating a crumb till we meet the kid most people would forget."

And when the little brother—David, the sheep watcher and goat herder and puny kid brother—came running in from the fields, Samuel exercised his eyes and imagined turning him inside out so he could see his heart. David's heart was far more beautiful than what people could see with their eyes.

And God said: "This is the one I picked to be king."

Long after that forgotten little son of Jesse was anointed king in Bethlehem, there was another unseen One born in that very same little town of Bethlehem—One who was left out with the sheep because no one made room for Him either.

Jesus was the most beautiful One who came down so our ugly hearts might become beautiful in the eyes of God.

Can you see it right now? Like you can almost see beyond the wrapping paper everywhere—to all the gifts inside. Those gifts are inside all of us, our hearts shimmering like stars.

Thoughts to Discuss

What kind of heart did David have? What's the one thing you can do to have the kind of heart you'd like to have?

Would you rather get a beautifully wrapped empty box or a wonderful gift in shabby wrapping paper? How is that like the way we should see other people?

Family Activity

How can you look at the inside of people instead of the outside? Say a prayer together, asking God to help you see others the way He sees them.

The people who walk in darkness will see a great light.

ISAIAH 9:2

DECEMBER 14

A Candle in the Darkness

Today's Reading: Isaiah 9:2, 6-7
The people who walk in darkness
will see a great light.
For those who live in a land of deep darkness,
a light will shine. . . .
For a child is born to us,
a son is given to us.
The government will rest on his shoulders.
And he will be called:
Wonderful Counselor, Mighty God,
Everlasting Father, Prince of Peace.
His government and its peace
will never end.
He will rule with fairness and justice from the throne of his ancestor David
for all eternity.
The passionate commitment of the Lord of Heaven's Armies
will make this happen!

Some dark night, turn out all the lights. Close your eyes. Then blindfold yourself. Is it really, really, really dark yet? Now, in the dark, with your eyes closed and completely blindfolded, walk from your bed to the kitchen. Without stubbing your toe! Without tripping! Without ever peeking, even once!

What would it be like if you had to walk around all your life in inky darkness all the time? What if you never stopped stumbling around in thick darkness everywhere, and no matter how you stumbled around, you could never find even a glimmer of light in the endless dark? What if you lived in a land of deep shadows that went on and on forever?

And then one day—bright white light! Fireworks of light! Explosions, sunbursts of light! Because in the middle of the land of deep and dark shadows, a Baby was born, a Baby who is God-in-skin, a Baby who was there when the sun itself was first ignited at the far edges of time. Because to you a Child is born, right into your dark and your sadness and sin, and Baby Jesus is Light Himself.

Jesus is the only real Light in the whole wide dark world. Turn to Jesus, and the light always turns on inside of you. For a Baby has been born, the only One who is blazing Light, and all the people who had been bumping around in the dark blink their eyes to the relief and the miracle of Light warming their faces, and they name the Baby. They come close to the only real Light in the whole world, and they name the Baby Amazing. Strong God. Eternal Father. (Yes, they name the Baby that, because under that fresh baby skin is the forever

Father God who is without end!) We don't have to stumble around in the dark, because Jesus is running the world. We don't have to be scared of the dark, because Jesus is our forever Light.

Jesus is our Light in the dark that we could never light with a match or flick on with a switch—Jesus is the Light we can only find.

Just like Christmas—Christmas can only be found.

Christmas cannot be bought in a store. Christmas cannot be created in the kitchen. Christmas cannot be made by hand, lit up, set out, dreamed up. Christmas can only be found—right there in the manger.

Christmas can only be found in the feed trough, in the muck, in the stench of a barn, and in

the unexpected—and only in the dawning light of Christ.

Our God who breathed stars into the dark—He breathed Bethlehem's Star, then He became a Baby with lungs and breathed in stable air. We are all saved and rescued from the hopeless dark because God came with infant fists and opened wide His hands to hold yours.

We are all saved from the dark of our loneliness because God is love and He can't stand to leave us by ourselves in the dark.

And it doesn't matter how dark the dark is—Jesus comes to the darkest places so you can see His light the brightest.

And now Jesus comes to be God with us, God in us, and He makes you to be a very real miraculous candle, a little light of joy and hope and love in the dark wherever you go.

The whole world is exploding in Christmas lights, for unto us a Child is born. And all the children round the world light up like the happiest candles of all!

Thoughts to Discuss

What does it mean to you that Jesus is our Light?

Who do you think needs His light today? How can you shine His light for them?

Family Activities

Light a candle and pray as a family for people you know who are hurting right now. Thank God for being the Light of the World.

As you hang today's ornament on your Jesse Tree, thank God that His light is brighter than any darkness.

How much longer will you waver, hobbling between two opinions? If the LORD is God, follow him!
1 KINGS 18:21

DECEMBER 15
Bowing Down

"I have made no trouble for Israel," Elijah replied. "You and your family are the troublemakers, for you have refused to obey the commands of the LORD and have worshiped the images of Baal instead. Now summon all Israel to join me at Mount Carmel, along with the 450 prophets of Baal and the 400 prophets of Asherah who are supported by Jezebel."

So Ahab summoned all the people of Israel and the prophets to Mount Carmel. Then Elijah stood in front of them and said, "How much longer will you waver, hobbling between two opinions? If the LORD is God, follow him! But if Baal is God, then follow him!" But the people were completely silent.

Then Elijah said to them, "I am the only prophet of the LORD who is left, but Baal has 450 prophets. Now bring two bulls. The prophets of Baal may choose whichever one they wish and cut it into pieces and lay it on the wood of their altar, but without setting fire to it. I will prepare the other bull and lay it on the wood on the altar, but not set fire to it. Then call on the name of your god, and I will call on the name of the LORD. The god who answers by setting fire to the wood is the true God!" And all the people agreed.

Many years after King David, God's people had an angry king named Ahab who didn't love God at all. Soon many of God's people also hated the one real God, who loved them with an unbeatable, unconditional, unwrappable love. Instead they worshiped a false, imaginary god they called Baal.

Now every heart beating in every person is made and wired to worship something. You might not be able to tell from the outside, but every one of us is bowing down to something. And if you don't choose to bow to the one real God, you'll bow down before a fake god—some Baal. See, Baal isn't just the name of one fake god; it's the name for anything we set our hearts on besides God. There's the Baal of bigger toys and the Baal of more stuff and the Baal of me, me, me. It's always our ugly Baals that keep us from the unstoppable, unfailing love of God.

So a man named Elijah—a man who loved God and listened to Him—told King Ahab to have everyone gather at Mount Carmel.

Elijah stood up at the front of the enormous crowd of people who were all bowing down to the Baals and cried, "How much longer will you lean this way and that way and flail and flop about between the one real God and the Baals? If the Lord is your one real God, follow Him and bow down to Him! But if some Baal is really what you are bowing down to, then don't pretend that God is your greatest Gift!"

They say that when you waver and flip-flop between two gods, what you are really doing is sinking, like you're drowning.

So Elijah told those Baal-bowers to put a bull on the altar and ask their Baal to light the whole thing up in a ball of fire. Then Elijah would do the same thing and pray to his God. Whichever one hurled down the fireballs was the one real God.

So the Baal-bowers built their altar, and then they flailed and flung about in this dance, trying to get Baal to drop down some fire. Then they started to do even more heartbreaking things like hurting and cutting themselves to get Baal to notice them, hear them, throw down some flame.

Can you guess how you know you're bowing down to a Baal on the inside? When you are trying to perform, trying to impress on the outside.

You know you have a Baal when you cut yourself down or cut anyone else down. Never forget the gift of it: there is only one real God who was cut open for you so your heart could be close to Him, so you don't cut yourself down or cut anyone else down.

But the Baal-bowers danced even more crazily, looking like they were drowning. It's hard to get a fake god to do anything for you, isn't it?

Then Elijah quietly poured water over his wooden altar—not once, not twice, but three times. Do you know how hard it is to try to start a fire with wood that's wet and dripping? And dripping and dripping?

But Elijah whispered, "Please send fire, one real God, so everyone will know you are the one real God." And fire fell like flaming stars out of the sky and lit the wet wood, the flames like tongues licking up the water ringing around the altar! (Was anyone expecting that?) The mouths of the people dropped shocked-open: the one real God is real.

Many years later, a star would burn like a glowing flame in the sky right over a stable where the little Baby God would lie in a manger much like an altar, and tongues would murmur it again that night, just like we do tonight: "The Lord is the one real God. He is really our God."

And you can feel it—this love for our Lord burning like a warming fire in all our hearts.

Thoughts to Discuss

How can you tell if something is a false god in your life? What are some Baals that have captured your heart?

Family Activities

Write down your Baals—your false gods—on little slips of paper. If you have a fireplace, toss the papers into the fire. If not, crumple them up and throw them away. Thank God that He is the one real God who is worthy of your worship.

As you hang today's ornament on the Jesse Tree, tell God that you choose to worship Him alone.

Go . . . and deliver the message I have given you.

JONAH 3:2

DECEMBER 16

Turning Around

The LORD gave this message to Jonah son of Amittai: "Get up and go to the great city of Nineveh. Announce my judgment against it because I have seen how wicked its people are."

But Jonah got up and went in the opposite direction to get away from the LORD. He went down to the port of Joppa, where he found a ship leaving for Tarshish. He bought a ticket and went on board, hoping to escape from the LORD by sailing to Tarshish. . . .

Now the LORD had arranged for a great fish to swallow Jonah. And Jonah was inside the fish for three days and three nights. . . .

Then the LORD ordered the fish to spit Jonah out onto the beach. . . .

Then the LORD spoke to Jonah a second time: "Get up and go to the great city of Nineveh, and deliver the message I have given you."

This time Jonah obeyed the LORD's command and went to Nineveh.

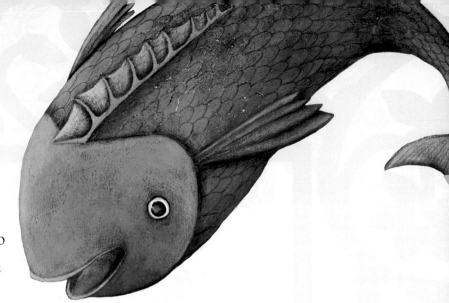

S ome days you just really don't want to
show up, you don't want to do the hard
things you have to do, and you don't want to
do the very big or even the very little things
that God tells you to do. Which is exactly
how Jonah felt when God asked him, "You know that city Nineveh?"

Jonah's eyes got big. "Nineveh? Where there are the meanest people *evah*?"

"Yes. That Nineveh." God smiled. "I want you to go to Nineveh and tell
the meanest people ever that I have the biggest love ever and they can choose
the unlovely, but My unbeatable, uncontainable, unconditional, unwrappable
love won't ever stop coming to undo all their very bad and very sad things."

Jonah thought about it for a whole two minutes—and ran as fast as he could
to find a one-way ticket to sail away from Nineveh.

But just as Jonah was drifting off for a nap on his gently rocking boat, the
rumble of a huge storm pitched him right out of bed.

Jonah woke up wide eyed. All around him, sailors were hurling bags and
blankets and barrels into the crashing waves, hoping to save the ship from going
down into the monster-dark sea. (Sometimes you have to let go of some things
to save the most important thing.)

But Jonah waved his arms. "What you have to toss in is me!"

The sailors raised their eyebrows like question marks. "Really?"

Jonah nodded. "It's the only way you can be saved."

So the sailors grabbed Jonah by his ankles, and the moment Jonah went *kerplunk* into the sea, the storm went *kerplop* down into the waves too.

Down, down into the watery silence Jonah fell—and right into the open mouth of a giant fish. *Gulp*. Jonah gulped hard—and the fish gulped him down.

And sitting there in the dark tomb-belly of the fish, Jonah got the gift that we all get in every storm: the gift of seeing how much we need God.

Sometimes it's only when you see that you have very little in your hands that you can take hold of God's very big hands. Could there ever be a bigger, better gift than getting more of God?

Jonah said sorry to God and turned around, right there in the turning and churning tummy of the fish. You always get the greatest gift when you turn around and go the right way, right toward the smiling ways of God.

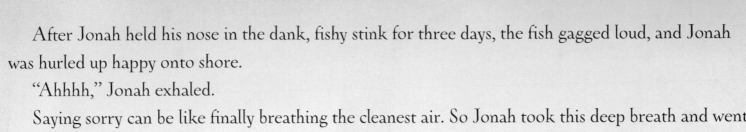

After Jonah held his nose in the dank, fishy stink for three days, the fish gagged loud, and Jonah was hurled up happy onto shore.

"Ahhhh," Jonah exhaled.

Saying sorry can be like finally breathing the cleanest air. So Jonah took this deep breath and went to Nineveh and told the meanest people ever that the greatest God ever loved them unconditionally and forever. And they turned around and ran right toward God and became the happiest people ever!

Little did Jonah know that nearly eight hundred years later, another Man would board a boat and sleep right through a rocking and rolling storm. And He'd wake up to friends whose eyes were big with fear. And that Man, Jesus, would whisper, "Someone greater than Jonah is here" (Matthew 12:41).

Because Jesus didn't calm just one storm but all our storms. Jesus throws Himself right into our angriest storms so He can calm our ugliest days. Since Jesus came to save us, there isn't a storm big enough to scare us.

What if you believed the miracle of a wild storm and a wilder resurrection right out of the belly of a

fish? What if you believed the even bigger miracle of God coming as a baby, God going to the Cross, and God rising from the dead—just like that, coming out of that tomb after three days? What if you believed in being raised from the angry belly of sin into the best day *evah*? Just go ahead and whisper sorry— and you will see the miracles start to happen!

Thoughts to Discuss

What's one thing you'd like to say sorry for?

How would you describe a miracle? Do you think miracles still happen today?

Family Activities

Write down something you want to tell God you are sorry about. Draw a heart around it to remind you that nothing can stop God's love for you.

As you hang today's ornament on your Jesse Tree, thank God for the miracle of forgiveness.

You, O Bethlehem Ephrathah, are only a small village.

MICAH 5:2

DECEMBER 17

A True Fairy Tale

TODAY'S READING: MICAH 5:2-5

You, O Bethlehem Ephrathah,

are only a small village among all the people of Judah.

Yet a ruler of Israel will come from you,

one whose origins are from the distant past.

The people of Israel will be abandoned to their enemies

until the woman in labor gives birth.

Then at last his fellow countrymen

will return from exile to their own land.

And he will stand to lead his flock with the LORD's strength,

in the majesty of the name of the LORD his God.

Then his people will live there undisturbed,

for he will be highly honored around the world.

And he will be the source of peace.

Have you ever gotten lost in the pages of fairy tales with their castles and kings? Well, once upon a time—which was actually before time began—a story began that is better than the most otherworldly fairy tale you've ever heard.

God gathered His children and told them what would happen even before it happened. The Father-King of the heavens and of all the universe and His Son-King looked across Their Kingdom and saw how all the children They had made were being held captive by the dark and the sinfulness and the sickness and the badness. They knew Their unconditional, unstoppable, unwrappable love had to come and get Their people us—so They came up with the very best rescue plan.

This is what They decided: the Father-King would open the back side of the world, and the Son-King would unexpectedly slip right into the Kingdom through a little, unlikely door: Bethlehem.

Remember Ruth, whose husband died? She followed Naomi back to nobody-would-be-expecting little Bethlehem, whose name means "house of bread." Many years later, Ruth's very own great-grandson, a puny little shepherd boy named David, spent many nights lying on the hills of Bethlehem, just staring up at the sea of blinking stars, his

heart beating with God's heart.

And then, long after King David, if you stacked one year up after another until you had a teetering tower of one thousand long years, the Son-King, Jesus, slipped into the Kingdom. He was born as a baby about as small as a little loaf of bread, right there in a barn in nobody-would-be-expecting little Bethlehem.

The moment the Son-King inhaled earth-air into His lungs, the blinding light of history slashed back the smothering dark, and the Son-King brought joy from beyond the walls of the world. And shepherds lying out on those same Bethlehem hills saw the sky bursting with a blinding star over little Bethlehem (because who would be expecting all that?).

The Son-King did not grow up in a palace—or even have a pillow to lay His head on. The Son-King had no throne or horse; He was a carpenter with a hammer. And He wandered the country-side fixing broken-down bodies and broken-up hearts, and breaking little loaves of bread to feed huge crowds of hungry people (because who would be expecting that?).

And then the Son-King let the very children He'd made and loved slap Him and whip Him and nail His always-loving hands to a cross. And all evil and badness across the universe laughed as if they'd won. Then they wrapped the Son-King's limp, dead body in rags and forgot Him in a grave. (Who ever expected the tears of all this?)

But then, when no one was expecting anything from another world at all, the Son-King jolted right up in the grave—alive!—and the light forever shattered the darkness. The King flung off the rotting grave clothes and rose, His perfect heart beating hope loud in His chest. Monster stones rolled (because who would be expecting that!). And the Son-King walked right out of that grave, His heel crushing the snakelike head of all the evil and badness, and all the King's children in the whole universe were wooed and wowed back to life again!

It's coming—the Kingdom's coming in little and small and unexpected ways. And the King is coming to rule the earth and make all the sad things untrue and make all the bad things come undone.

When we love in little ways, the big things unexpectedly begin to happen (they won't be expecting that!). In little places, through unexpected people, the story is unfolding and unwrapping all around you and in you, the light overtaking the dark. And it's like you can see the new Kingdom bursting in right now—how all the lit-up trees and all the trees of the field will clap their hands.

This story that is happening is better than the greatest fairy tale ever told—because it's all true.

Thoughts to Discuss

Why do you think Jesus was born in such a small, insignificant town?

How does it make you feel to know that God can do amazing things in little places with unexpected people?

Family Activities

Think of one little thing you can do today to make someone feel special.

I will go in to see the king.

ESTHER 4:16

DECEMBER 18

A Bridge to the King

Esther [said]: "All the king's officials and even the people in the provinces know that anyone who appears before the king in his inner court without being invited is doomed to die unless the king holds out his gold scepter. And the king has not called for me to come to him for thirty days." . . .

Mordecai sent this reply to Esther: "Don't think for a moment that because you're in the palace you will escape when all other Jews are killed. If you keep quiet at a time like this, deliverance and relief for the Jews will arise from some other place, but you and your relatives will die. Who knows if perhaps you were made queen for just such a time as this?"

Then Esther sent this reply to Mordecai: "Go and gather together all the Jews of Susa and fast for me. Do not eat or drink for three days, night or day. My maids and I will do the same. And then, though it is against the law, I will go in to see the king. If I must die, I must die."

Little Esther was an orphan—she had no father to hold her and no mother to help her. But she had an Uncle Mordecai to love her. And so love grew her up to be lovely. (Love is always what makes things lovely.)

Now King Xerxes was searching high and low throughout the entire kingdom, gathering up all the girls to see which one might be his new queen, when someone nudged lovely Esther forward. For months she waited with the other girls—waited for the king to call her name. For months Esther combed her long hair and rubbed oil into her smooth skin. But no one could see what made Esther's heart really beautiful: she really listened to people with her ears. She really looked into people with her eyes. What makes you beautiful is not how your face looks but how your heart loves.

When King Xerxes finally called Esther's name from his list, he looked up and saw this girl who shone. When King Xerxes placed the crown on beautiful Esther's head and whispered, "Queen!" he looked like he might burst into happy fireworks.

But one of the king's officers, Haman, hated Esther's uncle Mordecai. Haman's heart burned with such a hot anger that his mind scorched and smoked with a horrific idea—a law that would kill all God's children, just so he could get rid of Uncle Mordecai. But here's what neither Haman nor King Xerxes knew: Queen Esther was one

of God's children too!

After Uncle Mordecai heard the new law, he stood outside the palace gate and tore his clothes in half, because his heart was breaking in two.

He sent a message to Esther: "Really look into the eyes of God's children outside the palace gate. Really listen to the cries of God's children outside the gate. You, Esther, are the only one who can go to the king and help save us. This is the moment you were made for: to use your gifts to give others the gift of life."

It comes like a whisper from those outside the gate: *Use the life you've been given to give others life.*

Esther took a long, deep breath. If she went to see King Xerxes without his asking to see her . . . he could decide to have her killed! But Esther

imagined what it must feel like for God's children outside the gate. She could feel her beautiful heart thrumming it loud: *Use the life you've been given to give others life.*

So Esther decided—yes! She would be like a bridge from God's children to the king. When love for others makes your heart beautiful, it makes your hands brave. This is what Esther whispered: "I will go—and if I die, I die."

Then there's Jesus, the Son-King, whose home was the original palace, Jesus, who has the most beautiful heart in all the universe. Jesus thought of you when you were outside the gate, bruised and beaten up by sin. And His love for you was instant. He had to leave heaven—He had to risk everything to save you, to free you, to heal you. Like brave Queen Esther, Jesus made Himself a bridge back to the King. Jesus risked everything: "So I die, I die." And He saved us!

When you unwrap the unbeatable, unfailing, unstoppable love of Jesus, you laugh happiest: you are free, free, free to happily give away your gifts so other people can live. Right now, there's a boy digging for food in a garbage heap in India. Right now, a little girl is crying for food in Uganda. Right now, a child in

Afghanistan goes to sleep having never heard the name of Jesus. This is the moment you were made for: to use your gifts to give others the gift of life.

There could be unwrapping everywhere around the world! There's your heart, brave and beautiful and changing the world, giving love to the world, making the world dance with life and light and love.

Thoughts to Discuss

Do you think Esther was brave? Why or why not?

Do you think you need to be brave to share the greatest Gift with other people? Why or why not?

Family Activity

Think of a creative way you can tell others that God loves them. Be brave, just like Esther!

*I will climb up to my watchtower
and stand at my guardpost.
There I will wait to see what the LORD says.*

HABAKKUK 2:1

DECEMBER 19

Watch and Wait

I will climb up to my watchtower

and stand at my guardpost.

There I will wait to see what the LORD says

and how he will answer my complaint. . . .

Even though the fig trees have no blossoms,

and there are no grapes on the vines;

even though the olive crop fails,

and the fields lie empty and barren;

even though the flocks die in the fields,

and the cattle barns are empty,

yet I will rejoice in the LORD!

I will be joyful in the God of my salvation!

The Sovereign LORD is my strength!

He makes me as surefooted as a deer,

able to tread upon the heights.

The family tree of Jesus grew wider and bigger. Some were shepherds, and some were princesses, and some were kings. Then there was Habakkuk, who was a prophet. (Now a prophet is someone who listens carefully to what God says and gives God's message to God's people.)

Habakkuk climbed to the top of the watchtower—his special lookout place where he could see the whole city. He looked out over God's children and swallowed down his sadness. It cracked a bit of his heart. "Lord," he said, "people are using their words like weapons instead of as gifts for one another. People are using their hands to hurt each other instead of to help each other. People are forgetting that having You is more than enough—they are forgetting that You are the greatest Gift ever. So they are sinning greatly and are sadder than ever. Please do something!"

And God drew near—because that's what the one real God does. And God said, "Watch and wait, because the thing that is coming . . . well, no one will be expecting *this*!"

Would God come soon enough? Would God's plan really work? Would everything really be all right? Habakkuk's lips quivered a bit, and his knees trembled more than a bit. But God's unstoppable, unbeatable, unconditional love chases away all fears, and God's love made Habakkuk brave. Just like the cold can move you closer toward the fire, hard things can move you closer toward God. And He warms

you with joy.

Habakkuk shouted it from the top of the watchtower: "I will trust You, God, and I will watch, and I will wait. I will find joy, make joy, take joy, see joy! Rejoice and re-joys again!"

Then Habakkuk sang this song: "Even though the fig trees have no blossoms, even though there are hard things, even though I fail sometimes—I will be joyful in God. He saves us from the sadness and darkness and ourselves!"

Habakkuk was one of the smart ones who sang on, because even when there are hard things, there are happy things too—gifts from God! Warm hugs. Morning sunshine. Happy moon. You can count gifts all around you and recount gifts and rejoice. Re-joys! Joy in God is what makes you strong, so if you let that something steal your joy, you're letting it steal your strength!

Soon the angels would sing this song too: "Fear not! For behold!" All our fears are solved in the gift of Christmas. "Fear not! For behold!"

You have the greatest Gift: a Savior who really does save you! Since God gave even His own Son, won't He also give us everything else that we need (Romans 8:32)? Because God gave you Jesus, you can always give God all your trust! You can take your hands off the steering wheel of your life—you don't have to try to save yourself.

See and behold the love of Jesus everywhere, and you are held.

Quick, up to the top of the watchtower—and count all the everyday gifts! Soon, soon we will see the unwrapping of the greatest Gift of all!

Thoughts to Discuss

Is there something that has been stealing your joy lately? What has helped you get through sad times in the past?

Go around the room and have each person tell about a gift from God he or she noticed today.

Family Activity

Find a jar to use as your "grateful jar." Write down some of the things you are thankful for and put the slips of paper in the jar. Whenever you're having a rough day, you can empty the jar to remember the things you have to be grateful for.

He will prepare the people for the coming of the Lord.
LUKE 1:17

DECEMBER 20

God Remembers

Zechariah and Elizabeth were righteous in God's eyes, careful to obey all of

the Lord's commandments and regulations. They had no children because

Elizabeth was unable to conceive, and they were both very old.

One day Zechariah was serving God in the Temple,

for his order was on duty that week. . . .

While Zechariah was in the sanctuary, an angel of the Lord appeared to

him, standing to the right of the incense altar. Zechariah was shaken and

overwhelmed with fear when he saw him. But the angel said, "Don't be

afraid, Zechariah! God has heard your prayer. Your wife, Elizabeth, will

give you a son, and you are to name him John. You will have great joy and

gladness, and many will rejoice at his birth, for he will be great in the eyes

of the Lord. He must never touch wine or other alcoholic drinks. He will

be filled with the Holy Spirit, even before his birth. And he will turn many

Israelites to the Lord their God. He will be a man with the spirit and power

of Elijah. He will prepare the people for the coming of the Lord."

Now was the time when all the miracles began.

After speaking to prophets like Habakkuk and Malachi, God fell quiet. For a very, very long time. For four hundred long, long years, God's children looked up to heaven and could have heard a pin drop.

It had been five hundred years since anybody had seen angels. It had been six hundred years since Shadrach, Meshach, and Abednego walked through the flames with a fourth blazing angel from heaven.

But then, all of a sudden, it was like hundreds of quiet years shattered, and God's voice reverberated loud in hearts.

There he was—an angel appeared right in front of one old man. A certain wrinkled and graying priest named Zechariah. A priest who was shocked that his name had been drawn to offer the incense in the holiest place in the Temple. It was a special day that came only once a year: the Day of Atonement, the day when people celebrated being made right with God. Throughout a priest's whole life, his name might never be drawn to go into the holiest place. And once it was drawn, it could never be drawn again. This was Zechariah's big day.

Zechariah's name means "God remembers." But some days Zechariah felt like God had forgotten him. Everybody else had the gift of a child—but not Zechariah. Zechariah had no little boy of his own to play with, to love on, to dream with. Zechariah did have a wife. Her

name was Elizabeth—it meant "God's promise." Elizabeth prayed with Zechariah that God would remember, that He would remember His promise of a child. What more could anyone want than the miraculous gift of a child? Zechariah and Elizabeth prayed to believe that God remembered, that God kept His promises. This is always the best place for miracles to happen: God meets us right in the place where it's hard to believe. When our believing sort of runs out, God's loving always runs on.

Nothing is impossible with God!

This is what the angel declared: Zechariah ("God remembers") and his wife, Elizabeth ("God's promise"), would give birth to a baby boy who would be named John (which means "God is gracious"). That's the miracle that we all get! God gives us grace—He graciously gives us one gift after another. He gives us breath and life and each other, and He gives us all of Himself!

The angel told Zechariah, who could hardly believe it, "Your boy, John, will be a man with the spirit and power of Elijah." (Remember Elijah and the fireballs that fell straight from heaven? The time of miracles was here!)

This is what the angel said: "John will help people get their hearts ready for the coming of the greatest Gift ever!" That's really all we have to get ready for Christmas—our hearts. We need to get our hearts ready to welcome Jesus into every part of our lives. And guess how you best get your heart ready for Jesus? Come to Him just as you are.

It's like your name has been drawn! And you get the miracle of Christmas! You get more than just proof that God exists—you get the gift of really knowing God's presence.

You always get the greatest Christmas miracle. You get God with you!

God gives Himself as the greatest Gift, and He doesn't keep any truly good thing from you. Because the greatest things aren't ever things!

God never, ever withholds the greatest Gift from you—Jesus! Jesus is all good, and He is all yours, and this is always your miracle—your greatest Gift. And the best thing is that you can always have as much of Jesus as you want!

Can you feel the miracles beginning already?

Thoughts to Discuss

Have you ever experienced a miracle? Have you heard about someone else who experienced a miracle?

Why do you think the miracle of Christmas is one of the greatest miracles of all?

Family Activities

As a family, sing a Christmas song that reminds you of the miracle of Christmas.

Prepare the way for the LORD's coming!

MATTHEW 3:3

DECEMBER 21

Thunder in the Desert

In those days John the Baptist came to the Judean wilderness and began preaching. His message was, "Repent of your sins and turn to God, for the Kingdom of Heaven is near." The prophet Isaiah was speaking about John when he said,

"He is a voice shouting in the wilderness,

'Prepare the way for the LORD's coming!

Clear the road for him!'"

That boy of Zechariah and Elizabeth's grew up to be gloriously different from the rest of the crowd. John wore coats made of camel hair (no one was expecting that!). And he never let scissors get anywhere near his long hair. Or his bushy beard. John was a hairy kind of guy who lived out among the cactuses and the bushes of the desert. He snacked on grasshoppers (*crunch, crunch*). And he ate lots of wild honey. (Can you imagine all that wild honey, dripping into his long beard? Sweet!)

John was a bit like his dad, Zechariah the priest. John was a preacher—a preacher with only one message. He played his one message on repeat, and it was as simple and as special as John's simple, special life: "Change your ways, open up your arms, open up your hands, and say yes to God! Because God's Kingdom is here. The Son-King, Jesus, is coming!"

It was already happening. God was opening the back door of the universe—Bethlehem. The great rescue was starting! The love that had been coming for us ever since the beginning was coming to undo all the bad things. The Son-King was coming to rescue us from being captive to all the sinfulness and badness. Could there be a greater gift than an unbeatable, unstoppable, unwrappable love like this—a love that forever frees us?

John was so excited about this love, he couldn't keep quiet! He kept booming out the good news, just like he was thunder in the desert. (Who would be expecting that—thunder in

the desert?) Can you imagine how beautiful thunder
in the desert sounds? Thunder! Rain coming! All the dry land opening up its
thirsty cracks, ready to drink, drink, drink all the cool water that's coming! New
life! Blooming!

John thundered the joy of it: "Clear the road! Prepare the way! The Son-King,
Jesus, is coming!" The one real God, who breathed out stars beyond our galaxy
and is as pure and holy as a white flame, was coming. He is your saving God, your
rescuing God, your heavy-lifting God.

Clear the way, so nothing you want stops you from seeing Jesus. Clear the
road, so you don't let anything distract you from seeing His coming. Prepare the
way, not for more things, but for the greatest thing: Jesus is coming!

Jesus is coming to carry the heaviness and to wash away all the badness and to
give us the gift of happiness. Jesus makes us all happy—the happiness of kids all
tickled giddy! Because Jesus loves us 100 percent before we even do one percent,
because Jesus wants us 100 percent before we even do .01 eensy-weensy percent.

In these starry days before Christmas, all the mamas and all the grandmas, all
the old men and all the young men—we all get to be like kids, happy like only kids
get to be happy. We all get to be close and laugh together loud and love big and
rest smiling, because it's almost time. We get to love this better-than-a-fairy-tale
love story about a coming King who will make a way right through the wildernesses

and through walls to set us free to be happy forever with Him.

Everything is almost ready for Christmas now—because all we have to do is be awed and wowed that Jesus is always close to us, that He's the Gift we always get.

Do you feel it, coming down like a gentle rain, like a gentle snow? It's the wonder of Jesus coming down like love all around us, everywhere.

Thoughts to Discuss

What's one thing you could do to prepare the way for Jesus' coming now?

Family Activity

Spend some time today thinking about what it means to have Jesus here with you. How does He make a difference in your life?

Greetings, favored woman! The Lord is with you!

LUKE 1:28

DECEMBER 22

Wide-Awake Dreams

TODAY'S READING: LUKE 1:28-35, 38

Gabriel appeared to [Mary] and said, "Greetings, favored woman!

The Lord is with you!"

Confused and disturbed, Mary tried to think what the angel could mean.

"Don't be afraid, Mary," the angel told her, "for you have found favor with

God! You will conceive and give birth to a son, and you will name him

Jesus. He will be very great and will be called the Son of the Most High.

The Lord God will give him the throne of his ancestor David.

And he will reign over Israel forever; his Kingdom will never end!"

Mary asked the angel, "But how can this happen? I am a virgin."

The angel replied, "The Holy Spirit will come upon you, and the power of

the Most High will overshadow you. So the baby to be born will be holy,

and he will be called the Son of God." . . .

Mary responded, "I am the Lord's servant. May everything

you have said about me come true." And then the angel left her.

This is the story about Joseph (the many-many-great-grandson of David, the puny shepherd boy) and Mary, the girl he was engaged to. (Aren't family trees places where we find the most unexpected gifts?) One morning Mary turned around, and right before her very eyes, she saw the stuff of dreams—even though she was wide awake! A very real angel was standing in front of her. His name was Gabriel.

Gabriel beamed. "Good morning!" Mary was so surprised.

"You're beautiful with God's kind of beauty," he said. "The kind of beauty that makes a heart lovely because it really listens and really looks and really loves."

Mary was so shocked that her knees sagged a bit, like limp noodles.

"Mary, you have nothing to fear and everything to rejoice about," Gabriel assured her. "God has a gift for you—a gift for the whole world. You're going to have a baby boy! You will name Him Jesus, and He will be great—the greatest!" The very big plan of the Father-King to rescue us all was unfolding—it was unwrapping!

And Mary? Mary opened her hands (which is what a willing yes always does). Mary said yes to becoming a space for God.

Right there in the space beneath Mary's beating heart would come the beating love of God.

The Son-King, Jesus, who laid out the paths for all the stars, chose to fold Himself up small and lie in the space of Mary.

When you make space in your words, in your wants, in your ways for Jesus, He comes and lives in the most miraculous way in your heart, too.

It's the strangest, most wondrous thing: when you open up your hands and say yes to whatever God wants to give you, you are really holding on to the hands of God. And no matter what your day looks like, no matter what happens, no matter how bad things get, your very big God can make anything, no matter how bad, into a gift.

Right now, God wants to hold your unsure hand.

Right now, He wants to hold you and all your needs.

Right now, He wants to hold you and all your fears.

Right now, He wants to whisper gently, "I'm here—you have nothing to fear and everything to rejoice about. Nothing is impossible for Me! I promise I have good gifts for you—unbeatable love and unstoppable joy and unfailing strength and the most unwrappable Gift: Jesus, the Son-King, who always rescues you with the strongest arms of love!"

When we really listen to the heart of the sad kid down the street, when we really look into someone's loneliness and reach out with a letter, a hand, a surprise, we make a space for the amazing gift of Jesus in us. When we become a safe space for someone, we get the miracle of being a miraculous space for Jesus, too.

Now Mary's smile stretched almost off her face. Nothing is impossible for God! We can make space for Jesus to be in us! Mary nodded happy and

whispered, "I will help God give His love out to the world." It is the strangest wonder: you get far more happiness when you give than when you get.

Christmas is close now. Only one thing is necessary—just let your hands and your heart be a space for love to come into the world.

Soon Mary's Baby will come. Soon a velvet hush will fall over everything like a starry blanket over a waiting child.

Even now, we can wake up to the greatest dream and start giving the love. Even now, angels dance with joy.

Thoughts to Discuss

Is there anything you need to take a break from for a while to make more space for Jesus?

Family Activity

Close your hands in fists and then open them again. As you do, think about giving God whatever is bothering you. Find one way to open your hand and say yes to God.

DECEMBER 23

He Can't Stay Away

TODAY'S READING: MATTHEW 1:20-23

An angel of the Lord appeared to [Joseph] in a dream.

"Joseph, son of David," the angel said, "do not be afraid

to take Mary as your wife. For the child within her was conceived

by the Holy Spirit. And she will have a son, and you are

to name him Jesus, for he will save his people from their sins."

All of this occurred to fulfill the Lord's message through his prophet:

"Look! The virgin will conceive a child!

She will give birth to a son,

and they will call him Immanuel,

which means 'God is with us.'"

Joseph the carpenter didn't look up from his hammering one morning to find the angel Gabriel, like Mary did. No angel took the saw out of Joseph's hand to tell him that earth and heaven and holy fire were all meeting in his Mary and that God was coming as a Baby. No angel held the nails for a moment to tell Joseph that the Father-King of the universe, who cups the ocean depths in the hollow of His hand, would fold Himself small inside the safe space of Mary to grow bones and skin and a heart like ours.

No, one night after Joseph laid down his hammer and his nails and his saw and crawled tired under the covers, he simply closed his eyes. He drifted far out into the black sea of sleep, where all of a sudden an angel flashed into his dream.

"Joseph," the angel told the many-many-great-grandson of David, "go ahead and marry that girl Mary, with the heart full of beauty and the hands that stretch out open. She's expecting a Baby—and the Baby is God!"

Who ever expected that?

"Now, Joseph," the angel said, "you get the job of naming the Baby Boy. Don't name Him any of the names in all the branching, reaching family tree—not Abraham or Isaac or Jacob or Boaz or David—because this Baby is God and man. You will name Him Jesus, because it means 'the Lord saves.' This Baby is the One the whole epic story of the universe, the tale of the greatest rescue, has been leading up to. He's finally coming to save His children from the badness and selfishness and sinfulness that held them captive to the darkness. So you will name Him 'the Lord saves—God is with us.'"

That better-than-a-fairy-tale story was now being delivered, and bringing our delivery—delivering us into freedom!

Joseph couldn't sleep for the excitement! The words rang in him like a hammer:

Jesus. Will. Save.

God. With. Us.

God with us!

He is the God who is so for you that He can't stay away from you! The God who so loves you and likes you and isn't merely a little bit for you or halfway for you or kind of for you but is always, fully, completely, totally, entirely, all the way, 100 percent for you—this is the God who chooses to be right *with* you.

So God threw open the door of this world and entered as a Baby.

He came as a Baby because He was done with the barriers.

He disarmed Himself so that you could take Him in your arms. God came as a Baby because He wants to be unimaginably close to you.

What God ever came so tender that we could touch Him? So fragile that we could break Him? Only the One who loves you to death. Only the God who had to come back to get you, to free you, to be with you.

Who wants the gift of His presence more than anything else?

Christmas isn't about getting something big and shiny. It's about God's doing whatever it takes to be with us—and our doing whatever it takes to be with Him.

There are candles to be lit. There are Christmas carols to sing. See how even the stars seem to be moving nearer now?

Hear it everywhere, the best news of all: "God is with us! God is with us!"

Those words ring like a hammer, like singing, like love building unbelievable things.

Thoughts to Discuss

Do you remember what Jesus' name means? Why do you think God decided that His name should mean "the Lord saves"?

When is it hardest for you to remember that God is with you?

Family Activity

Find out what each member of your family's name means. Create a reminder of the meanings of their names.

She . . . laid him in a manger, because there was no lodging available for them.

LUKE 2:7

DECEMBER 24

Kneel at the Manger

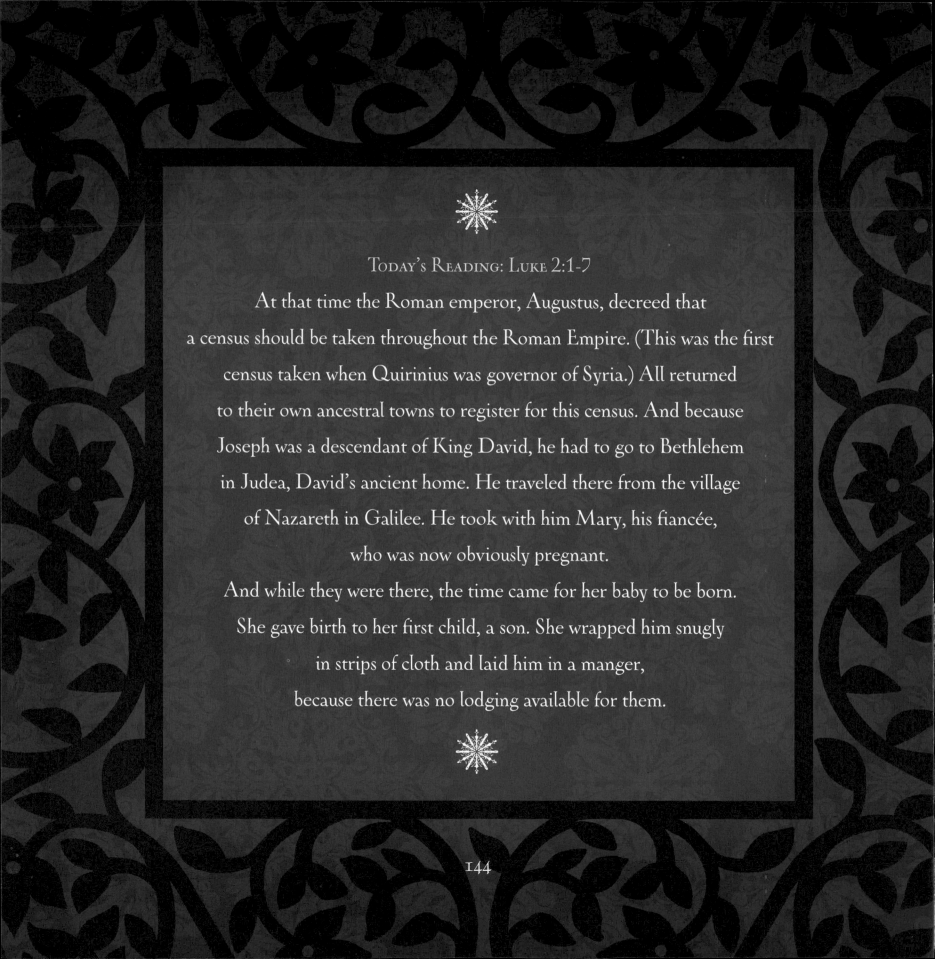

TODAY'S READING: LUKE 2:1-7

At that time the Roman emperor, Augustus, decreed that
a census should be taken throughout the Roman Empire. (This was the first
census taken when Quirinius was governor of Syria.) All returned
to their own ancestral towns to register for this census. And because
Joseph was a descendant of King David, he had to go to Bethlehem
in Judea, David's ancient home. He traveled there from the village
of Nazareth in Galilee. He took with him Mary, his fiancée,
who was now obviously pregnant.
And while they were there, the time came for her baby to be born.
She gave birth to her first child, a son. She wrapped him snugly
in strips of cloth and laid him in a manger,
because there was no lodging available for them.

The time is here! It's here! All of heaven, all the angels, all the span of history has been waiting just for this.

God turned one last time as a Baby inside of Mary, and then the skin of very God slipped naked and small into hands that He Himself had made.

This is the birth of God—who can find words?

Mary and Joseph hunched in a stable, awestruck that they were holding in their trembling hands the Son-King, who is the Father-King's rescue plan to free His children from badness and darkness. Mary and Joseph could hardly breathe in this scent of God with skin. The Lord saves. God with us. Jesus.

But remember how there is always more happening than we can see? And on the night Jesus was born, there was more happening than we could see. God's letter to us, the Bible, tells us that high, high up in the heavens, above the manger, behind the velvet curtain of silent stars, an all-out war flashed angry. Armies of evil exploded in a raging battle against God, the Father-King of the universe. In heaven, when Jesus was born, it wasn't a silent night; it was a cosmic war spinning across space. All of earth held its desperate, wild breath.

Jesus came for you, warring against the darkness to win you back to Him. The evil enemy of God, Satan, who tried to hold us all captive after our sinful fall in the Garden of Eden, fell like lightning from heaven—fell out of the sky in a heap.

And then, at last, all was calm. All was bright. Over Bethlehem the star hung high and victorious on that silent night, that holy night.

His love had to rescue you and release you to love. All the other love stories don't compare to this one—because this is the truest, realest story that ever was. This night, our rescue has come. God has visited our planet, and we can breathe free.

Jesus didn't enter the world in a palace or in a king's court. Instead, He chose to enter our world right in a pile of mucky, messy, stinky, dirty straw. Jesus comes and meets you in the stinky mess of your sin. Jesus comes to you small when you feel invisible and rejected. Jesus is with you now. Wherever you are, no matter what is happening, Jesus always wants to be with you. The Lord saves. Jesus is with us.

A love this unbeatable, unstoppable, unwrappable is a love that the mind can't fully understand. It can only be felt. Can you find the places inside you where you feel unwanted and unloved? You can be touched right there by Jesus. Do you know the places inside you where you feel small? Right there, you can reach out to Jesus. Come and kneel close. Let the warm breath of heaven fall on you.

Jesus waits to be held. Jesus waits for you to draw close.

Tonight, at the foot of the cradle of Christ, like at the foot of the cross of Christ, there are no big people, no powerful people, no proud people. Tonight we are all children who straggle to the manger with nothing. Tonight we are all just raggedy manger stragglers—fathers who lay down all their work, mamas who lay down all their weariness, children who lay down all their wants. Tonight we kneel down before Jesus and reach out our hands that need little—because we want more of God.

Tonight we're just raggedy manger stragglers who feel the heaviness of our old raggedy clothes from fighting the long battle with evil and badness. With our raggedy rags, we've tried to polish this dark world into something good enough to win our way to freedom. With our raggedy rags, we've tried to patch together our own ropes to somehow climb to freedom. With our raggedy rags, we've tried to disguise ourselves as someone else, as someone better, as someone bigger, thinking we could sneak our way to freedom and back to God.

Jesus whispers, "The freedom you could never earn with your raggedy rags—that's what I came to give you. I came to win you back to Me, to give you Myself, to make you free. I did it for love, because I could never, no matter what, ever stop loving you."

And all of happy heaven and thankful earth echo tonight with Jesus, the God-Child who came for us: He did it for love.

What can all of us manger stragglers do but wrap Jesus close to our raggedy hearts so He can rest in our love? The greatest Gift has been laid into our waiting hands . . . our waiting hearts. Can you almost hear it? The sound of stars singing this perfect, freeing love over all of us manger stragglers tonight.

Thoughts to Discuss

How do you feel Jesus' love, His presence, with you everywhere you go? How can you keep unwrapping the gift of His presence—the gift of God with you?

Family Activity

Write a thank-you note or draw a picture, thanking Jesus for His unstoppable love. Write a note to a neighbor, sharing this love.

DECEMBER 25

Never-Ending Christmas

TODAY'S READING: LUKE 2:11-19

"The Savior—yes, the Messiah, the Lord—has been born today in

Bethlehem, the city of David! And you will recognize him by this sign:

You will find a baby wrapped snugly in strips of cloth, lying in a manger."

Suddenly, the angel was joined by a vast host of others—

the armies of heaven—praising God and saying,

"Glory to God in highest heaven,

and peace on earth to those with whom God is pleased." . . .

[The shepherds] hurried to the village and found Mary and Joseph.

And there was the baby, lying in the manger. After seeing him, the shepherds

told everyone what had happened and what the angel had said to them about

this child. All who heard the shepherds' story were astonished, but

Mary kept all these things in her heart and thought about them often.

Doesn't today dawn differently? Isn't the light all different?

That's because the glory is rising—glory to God in the highest heaven, and peace to all the earth. God has left the glory of the galaxies and has come down to save us, to love us, to rescue us, to free us.

God is here! God is here! Jesus is born to you—to *you*! The glad tidings are to you—to *you*! It's like the sky is filling with a light that is different from the sun or the stars or anything of this world.

It's like one star leaned too close to the glory and majesty of the God-become-Baby and blew up bright.

The flame of it lit up the shepherds on the hills, and they blazed bright too, full of wonder. Those shepherds ran all the way to the manger, where even the fiery star seemed dim next to the brilliance of Jesus, the Light of the World.

All over the world right now, a thousand thousand trees dance with light.

All over the world right now, a thousand thousand gifts are given.

All over the world right now, at the foot of every tree, we are all unwrapping love.

Jesus, the Son-King, who made everything in this universe, gives you the sun to warm your skin and the moon to make a bright door in the sky. Jesus gives you the stars to dance glory over you, and He gives you a whole sky of air for you to breathe in, to fill your lungs with realest life.

Everywhere, everywhere—there are gifts everywhere from Jesus. Gifts are our air.

And when we sin and fall and trip and aren't happy with what God gives (that's what sin is: thinking God isn't enough), Jesus never stops loving us. He comes and gives us Himself.

That's what Jesus is whispering to you this Christmas Day: "I'll take your broken heart and give you My whole one."

Isn't that the most amazing, greatest Gift? You can always have as much of Jesus as you want! Your heart could burn hot with a love like this.

Our whole grand, epic story, right from the beginning, has been about Him. And when people see that it's all about Jesus, this is what they whisper: "Wasn't it like our hearts were on fire right inside of us?" (Luke 24:32).

Can you see it? This day, this night, the Light comes! Can you feel it? Your heart kindling, burning with a love for Jesus that's like a warming fire.

Now the shepherds out in the hills of Bethlehem that night had angels come to them, lighting their hearts on fire. But no one else heard angels—everyone else only heard the news from the hearts-burning shepherds. When your heart burns with love for Jesus, you're like a flaming match that lights up all the other hearts with the news of Jesus.

When you're just one of the raggedy manger stragglers who comes with nothing but your raggedy heart to Jesus, when you lean in close over Jesus in that manger and you see His blazing glory, when you come close to His white-hot love for you—how can you not scramble right out of the manger and right into the world with a heart glowing like hot embers of love for Jesus, telling everyone about the love of Jesus? A heart that really loves Jesus could catch the world on fire with love and more love and more love.

It's true: Jesus came into the world for you! And it's really true: you came into the world for Him, to let everyone know about Him.

The whole world lingers long at Christmas trees tonight, not wanting Christmas to be over. All of us sit together, longing for this wonder to go on.

But somewhere one Christmas candle flames bright in the quiet. And it will never ever be dark again. "For unto us a Child is born, unto us a Son is given" (Isaiah 9:6, NKJV). God is with us. Jesus is with us. Jesus stays with us.

The Christmas candle burns hot tonight, giving its brilliant light, because Christmas goes on forever. Because we have Jesus with us—the greatest Gift of unfailing, unbeatable, unstoppable love that we can keep unwrapping all our days.

Thoughts to Discuss

What do you think it means that Jesus is the greatest Gift? How can you unwrap more of Him in the coming year?

Family Activity

As you hang the final ornament on your Jesse Tree, celebrate and feel the burning warmth of the love of Jesus in your heart! Thank Jesus for being your greatest Gift—and pray that He will help you light this world on fire with His warming love.

Also by Ann Voskamp

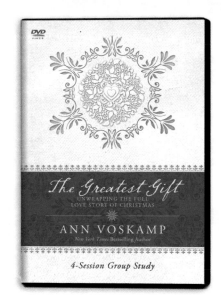

THE GREATEST GIFT
Perfect for personal reflection and daily devotions

THE GREATEST GIFT DVD CURRICULUM
Designed for families, small groups, and Bible study classes

As you and your family celebrate the coming of Christ this Advent season, I invite you to download the exquisitely designed ornaments featured in this book from my website to adorn your own Jesse Tree. I pray they will be a perennial reminder of the true miracle of Christmas and of God's greatest Gift to us.

—*Ann Voskamp*

www.aholyexperience.com

(Use code JESSE)

Experience
The Greatest Gift
in your home

Order your very own set of Jesse Tree ornaments today.

NEW this year from (in)courage, two wonderful companion ornament sets are being offered online.
Order your very own set or give as a gift this Christmas season.

Sculpted Resin Ornaments
in keepsake packaging

Embossed Paper Ornaments

For more information or to order your set today go to www.dayspring.com/greatestgift

Follow us on twitter @incourage

CP0805